Fe[illegible]e Friendship GUIDE

The no-holds-barred guide to celebrating, navigating, and strengthening your female friendships

Emilia Stypulkowska and Yvonne Rodney

Female Friendship Guide

ISBN-13: 978-1-990476-07-5
Published by: Expert Author Press
https://www.expertauthorpress.com/

Canadian Address:
1908 – 1251 Cardero Street,
Vancouver, BC, Canada, V6G 2H9
Phone: (604) 941-3041
info@expertauthorpress.com

Disclaimer

The focus of this book is exclusively on female friendships. While many of the friendship issues we discuss relate to men, we believe that women have unique ways of navigating their friendships. We have also spotted patterns regarding issues that tend to emerge with female friendships.

To that end, our examples and solutions are targeted specifically at women in hopes that they will help us to maintain, celebrate, and better understand our treasured friendships.

Names have been changed or omitted to protect and preserve confidentiality and privacy.

Foreward

Sisters. BFFs. My girls. Squad. Support team. Posse. Confidantes. Whether we have one best friend or a cluster, many women cannot imagine life without them. These women who comprise our support system, how did they get there?

Our friendships are as complex as the personalities and histories that make up each relationship. And while it might not be an initial consideration for starting a friendship, all of us come into our relationships with a wish, a desire, or a set of expectations. We like when someone gets us, is there for us, supports us, and cheers us on. This is especially true for the women we choose as our friends.

Even though no formal contract was signed to pledge our ongoing allegiance or fidelity, we count on the security and understanding our female friendships provide. And when our women friends betray our trust–it can feel like the Ultimate betrayal.

The paths to female friendships are as diverse as the 110 women who responded to our female friendship questionnaire (see Appendix A) and provided their viewpoints. In this book, we will meticulously parse and report on their perspectives and our own. We will delve into what they have shared about sustaining this important aspect of our lives as women, creating and nurturing our female friendships, voiced or unvoiced expectations, navigating conflict, and knowing if it's time to say goodbye.

And because this book is not about women in general but about us, we, the authors, have chosen to integrate our voices with yours. We will join in the conversation as if at a round table—a collective friendship circle—participating, listening, observing, learning, and sharing.

But more than anything, this book is about celebrating the abundant joy and steady support of great female friends and imparting lessons and advice from women to women.

"I am blessed beyond belief to have you in my life. I am grateful every day that we met, because if it were not for you and what you bring to my life, I would not be the person I am today"

Table of Contents

Why Female Friendships?

"You motivate me every day to want to do better. Thanks for not judging me when I judge myself. When I'm down, you are always there to pick me up, encourage, listen, and when I don't want to talk, you are still there even to sit in silence."

Aren't all friendships, regardless of gender, basically the same and provide the same benefits and challenges? Or are there different dynamics at play in friendships between women? If yes, what are they, and what can we learn from them?

What's So Special About Female Friendships?

We agree that many aspects that are effective and relevant to relationships are also applicable to female relationships. However, we also believe that female friendships have qualities that are unique and special, and these qualities are worth delving into and exploring. That's why we chose to tackle a book on this topic and sought feedback from other women.

We asked women about the length of their friendships, how many people comprised their friendship circle, the benefits of these friendships, the challenges, how they maintained their friendships, how they communicated, what they valued, and much more. 110 women between the ages of 20-70+ years shared their perspectives in eloquent, passionate, strong, cautionary, and heartfelt words.

If you've picked up this book, perhaps it's because you also have a perspective on this topic and want to see how it compares to the views of other women. Or perhaps you want to learn how to be a better friend, become more intentional about your friendships, or make new friends. Before delving too specifically into the subject of female friendships, let's take a step back and examine the question of what draws us to people in general.

What Draws Us to People?

Because humans are social beings, we form friendships, tribes, circles, clubs, groups, and communities. But what makes us select certain people over others? Social psychologists studying the concept of interpersonal attraction purport that the people who become part of our chosen 'inner circle' arrive in our lives through various ways and means. Here are some of the prevalent explanations:[1]

- **Proximity:** We tend to befriend those who are geographically near us. These are the people in our workplaces, neighbourhoods, schools, fitness classes, places of worship, etc. We see them often. Their nearness allows us to get to know them better.

[1] Berscheid, E. & Walster, E.H. Interpersonal Attraction, 2nd Edition (1978) Addison-Wesley Publishing Company.

- **Similarity:** We tend to like people who look like us, think like us, and dress like us. In the company of people similar to us, we feel affirmed.
- **Social Approval:** We tend to like those who like us and dislike those who dislike us. When we are with people who like us, it makes us feel confident.
- **Reinforcement:** We favour those who reward us and stay far away from those who punish us or put us down. While each person may differ in what is considered rewarding or punishing, we tend to keep people in our inner circle of friends because they provide something that we want or need.
- **Avoiding Social Isolation:** Because humans are social beings, we suffer from prolonged social isolation. Instead, we enjoy being around people who make our lives more pleasant, walk alongside us, share our fears and stresses, and support us during difficult times.
- **Cooperation:** We prefer those who cooperate with us and dislike those who compete with or frustrate our plans. In other words: If you are not for me or with me, you are against me.

In reviewing these explanations, we can see how some, if not all, of the women friends in our lives fit at least into one or more categories. What we want to do in this book is go beyond the factors that drew us into our friendships and examine what we can do to navigate, maintain, strengthen, and deepen them.

As stated earlier, we, the authors, will fully participate in this conversation and add our own stories, experiences, and opinions. After all, that's what girlfriends do!

Let's first hear from Emilia.

Emilia

I was destined to go through life with a best friend. I was born into my first best friendship. My sister is a mere year and a half older than I am. Growing up, we shared a love of many things like books, talking, and TV. We shared a room, so we spent most of our time together even when we didn't want to. I quickly grew accustomed to having someone by my side to confide in and discover the world with.

With that solid grounding at home, it's no wonder that I soon found a girl that I would call my best friend when I started elementary school. She and I sat together at lunch, traded sandwiches, and talked. That was the basis of our friendship, but we were bonded in my mind.

When I changed schools in middle school, I found myself a new best friend. We did everything together and were inseparable. We went on bike rides, listened to music, and talked about our crushes.

By the way, none of these friendships ever diminished my friendship with my sister. What changed was the additional person who held the oh-so-coveted title of 'best friend' in my life. I would happily declare that I had two best friends in my late teens. We planned out what we wanted from life: post-secondary schools, careers, and marriage, and we professed our intention to go through life by each other's sides.

When I reached my mid-twenties, one of these friendships got rocked by life changes, insecurities, and unexpressed conflict in a way that I hadn't imagined was possible in the utopian landscape of my best friendships. I had just moved five hours away from my hometown when my best friend called to tell me the fantastic news—she was engaged! She excitedly told me the story of her proposal, knowing that I would be thrilled for her. She and her boyfriend had been dating for five years, and I had seen them through their entire relationship up to that point. And to crown off this exciting news, she instantly named me her Maid of Honour!

We planned a visit for her and her fiancé to my new city so that we could all celebrate together. I was so proud and happy when they came to visit. I made a fuss and took lots of pictures to capture their happiness. But as the plans for the wedding progressed, insecurity grew inside of me. A low-grade anxiety resided about my own life. I was in a long-term relationship, but I constantly doubted whether my boyfriend and I would one day get married. I wasn't even confident we'd be together long enough for him to be my date for my friend's wedding! I had always wanted to get married and have a family of my own. My best friend's life was a subconscious benchmark, and I was falling behind.

Still, I pushed ahead with the wedding-related events with all the enthusiasm I had in me. But my insecurities about my own life continued to grow. I tried my best to offer the excitement and support my friend deserved, but my energy was waning, and my resentment was mounting. She was feeling let down, and I was feeling unappreciated. But we never talked about it. Those unexpressed feelings lingered and eroded our closeness.

Eight years have passed since my best friend's wedding. I have seen her beautiful family grow and have been there for her in hard times. I love her wholeheartedly and believe our friendship will always be there. I think back to the time of her wedding and now see it as a perfect storm – one we hadn't seen coming or prepared for. I have learned so much since that time. I want to share what I've learned to help women navigate storms like ours and sustain their friendships through inevitable change.

My female friendships are and always will be my greatest treasures. I want to help women deepen the bonds in their lives and navigate (or avoid!) the issues that erode these bonds. My wish is that this book reminds us all that our female friendships are to be cherished, celebrated, and strengthened.

I dedicate this book to all my wonderful female friends. I am grateful to each of you for the love, support, loyalty, and understanding you have given me. Our friendships have been mirrors of my life, and thanks to you, I am grateful for the growth and development I have done as a person.

Reviewing Emilia's story, do you see any parallels to your own? Do you notice any themes or patterns? When Emilia reviewed her history, here is what she observed that facilitated the writing of this book:

My life has been blessed with many wonderful female friends, but these friendships have not been without struggle and conflict. This is proof that my friendships have a depth of love and meaning. I give my friendships a lot of energy, thought, time, and effort. I don't take it lightly when I have a conflict with one of my friends. I think about it, analyze it, discuss it, think about it some more, and maybe even read a book to learn about the issue and how to resolve it. Through discussion and dissection of the conflicts I've had with friends, I've realized that other women seem to encounter similar pitfalls and issues in their friendships. This is how I became so invested in this book's topic.

We do not want this book to be a clinical exercise. We want you to take it personally. We take it personally. Many were the debates and discussions we had together as we wrote.

Let's now see what Yvonne brings to the discussion.

Yvonne

I've always had female friends but never a best friend. I wanted that: a friend who was my exclusive go-to girl. But like most relationships, sometimes the person you'd love to be your friend doesn't feel the same way about you or is not prepared to make the friendship exclusive.

I came close once to having a friend like that in Grade 9. She was a tall, thin, bright girl with the same name as me. I knew I wanted to be friends with her when she bought a 2-pack of Hostess chocolate cupcakes (you know the ones with the creamy white center?), and she gave me a whole one (I still remember the taste of that moist chocolate on my tongue). We didn't see each other outside of school, but we spent all our time together when we were there.

At the end of the summer, three years into our friendship, I returned to school in September, only to learn that my friend was extremely ill. I had a chance to visit her, but unfortunately, she passed away shortly after. She was my first and only almost exclusive friend.

During my mid-teens to late twenties, I intentionally sought out male friendships. My female peers were too emotional, gossipy, competitive, and ultra-feminine for my taste. I did not share their interests and couldn't relate to what they considered important. As a result, I shied away from activities or events that were exclusively female-oriented. One day, against my better judgment, I allowed someone to persuade me to attend a women's conference. That experience reinforced why I didn't want to be around women as a group. Over the course of the two days, at one time or another, almost every woman at that conference ended up bawling her eyes out and telling strangers things about their lives that, to me, should not be shared. I observed it all with detached disdain and mentally pledged that I'd never be caught dead in that kind of environment again.

But as I navigated my thirties, became a wife and a mother, and got bounced around and challenged by life, I started to have a new respect and appreciation for the support and understanding offered to me by the women in my life. At this point, I revised my opinion of females as purely sappy emotional beings and decided to invest in these relationships. I discovered that women had much to teach me, that we had a lot in common, and that there were things I could share with my girls that I couldn't with my guy friends. Who would have thought!

As I reflect on my life to date, I would say that I have been blessed with three solid but distinct pockets of female friends who've journeyed through life with me. When we get together, the conversation is sweet, deep, and meaningful as we share, encourage, and bolster each other. We've also gotten into the habit of affirming each other by giving 'word bouquets,' which helps us appreciate one another and reminds us not to take each other for granted. I could not imagine life without these women whom I've turned to in times of crises, pain, and joy.

Extending from these three pockets of friends are other women who are part of me but not as close. We don't regularly talk on the phone, message, or go out to dinner, but they are there for the once-per-year meetups and group endeavours. We have moments of deep sharing surrounded by food, lots of laughter, and debates, but we have chosen to remain on the periphery of each other's lives. Our lives are busy, and friendships take work. I cannot be there to the same degree of intensity for all the women I know and would, had I the bandwidth, like to know better. So, I cling to these deep inner pockets of female friends who have stood the test of time and are still there, choosing to enrich my life with the precious gift of their friendship.

Sometimes, I still yearn for an exclusive BFF, but I think that ship has sailed. Choosing to become exclusive at this point would definitely put someone's nose out of joint, and I don't have the energy to juggle and pacify.

Instead, I reach out to the woman friend who can best meet my needs at the moment when I need an exclusive ear. Some are more emotionally supportive than others. Each has a gift for me in their friendship: a sharp voice of reason, a pot of soup or soul-restoring food, a passion for people when I might otherwise disengage, a kind word, and always laughter until our cheeks hurt.

I still lose patience with gossipy and emotional women, but I'm becoming more at peace with my emotional side. Life has allowed me to experience the heady relief of tears shed in the company of safe sisters. Now I run to them first. I offer to do speaking engagements for women's conferences. I write books about women's pain. I am privileged to tell our stories. And I know with profound certainty, even though our lives are busy, these inner pockets of female friends would drop everything for a time to be by my side if ever I'm in a pinch and call for help.

Nowhere in our coming together did we stand before God and witnesses and declare that we would love each other through bad times and good, when it is easy or difficult. At no time did we sign a contract of fidelity. But my-oh-my, through all the chapters of my life, there have been, and continue to be, women friends who've made my life so very rich.

Fidelity. An old word. But yes, my girls have been so very faithful to me.

Did you, like Yvonne, view female friendships with a certain degree of skepticism? Has that skepticism changed, or is it still there?

Yvonne summarized her own story this way:

I am an introvert. I want friends to be there for me, spend time with me, and be dedicated. But if I am to be truly honest, [and I challenge each of you to be as you read this book], I work against myself. I want closeness, and to be sought after by my friends, but I pull away at times.

Too many people, and too much neediness, dependence, or reliance, drain me. I want a friend who needs me, but not too much; who loves me but does not cloister me. When I don't have it, I crave it. And sometimes, when I get it, I shy away from it. So how then is a friend to interpret what I need? Am I fated to remain unfulfilled even as I am surrounded by the abiding presence of women who have supported me through the years? I am still a living bundle of contradictions: friendly, supportive, aloof, alone, warm, cold, shy, outgoing—to name a few.

Can you relate to Yvonne's tale of contradictions?

The Benefits of Female Friendships

Our respondents had a lot to say about the benefits of female friendships. The common thread that came up in the answers is that women want to connect with other women because they can be truly understood by those who experience what they experience—mood changes and period cycles, motherhood, menopause, childbirth, the emotions of motherhood, pregnancy, coping with the unique differences of their male partners, and the list goes on!

Some responses included similar struggles—some of which aren't unique to our biology but rather our shared experiences of being seen and treated as women—like solidarity, having a place to feel safe, understood, and accepted. Women described friendly intimacy without strings attached, receiving mental, emotional, and spiritual support, encouragement, and advice. They talked about how other women uplift them and how they could truly be themselves in the company of women without being afraid or feeling judged. Some felt women were similarly wired on an emotional level.

The list is fairly long, and the women filling out the questionnaire certainly weren't at a loss coming up with benefits! At the heart of these answers was the feeling of being understood by those who were similar and had similar life experiences, struggles, and quirks.

In succeeding chapters, we will look at our expectations of our friends, the roles we play, the conflicts that arise, and how to deal with them. We will use the data from 110 women like you who have the wisdom to share about the female friends they've had, kept, or lost over the years. And we hope, at the end of this no-holds-barred female friendship guide, we will all learn important lessons, gain insights, and find even more reasons to celebrate those women we've chosen to be part of our inner circle of girlfriends.

Key Learning

- Different factors draw us into friendships.
- There is something special about female friendships.
- All of us have a story and a perspective.

Discussion Questions

1. What is your intention for reading this book? What do you hope to learn?
2. What do you feel your female friendships have to offer in your life?
3. What kind of friend do you want to commit to being? Do you plan to verbalize this commitment?

Becoming Exclusive BFFs

"Thank you for being the wind at my back in the good and bad times. You have been on the path with me through life's journey for 37 wonderful years, and I wouldn't trade you for anyone. We have learned and grown through the many challenges and obstacles, but the one thing that never changes is the love, trust, and respect that we hold near and dear for each other. You will always be my ride or die best friend."

How Does a Friend Become a Best Friend?

Not everyone chooses to name someone a best friend. Many women have a few close friends and would never dream of singling one out, especially at the risk of offending them. It seems that best friendships usually form organically over time instead of being chosen arbitrarily over a group dinner.

Here's an example of how someone might become a best friend. Perhaps you have decided to start spending more time with one of your friends. There doesn't have to be a reason for this, but sometimes it's circumstantial. Maybe you live close to each other and have an easier time making plans spontaneously. Or perhaps you plan a trip or spend many of your weekends together. By seeing each other and talking frequently, you begin to know more about each other and maybe even start to develop inside jokes. You spend more time together, creating shared experiences and opportunities to bond.

When you spend a lot of time with this person, your trust grows. This might mean you disclose more about your life to them, creating further intimacy. It's also possible that a defining moment occurs in this close friendship that spurs its evolution. Perhaps you go through a tough breakup, and they check on you every day and make regular plans to help you get through that tough time. And then, at some point, one of you might introduce the other as their best friend or call the other that affectionately in conversation. And boom, that's it. That's how two friends might become official BFFs. It's not usually a complicated process, but its implications can be huge, especially over time.

Emilia

Over the years, my friendships have been similar to my dating life—I'm a serial monogamist. I usually have one person I spend more time with and have a closer relationship with.

When I entered high school, my best friendship with Gabriella was quite official. We named it that. In fact, her former best friend, the one she'd had since she was a kid, was jealous. We even had an awkward run-in at the mall one day with her former best friend and her boyfriend. The encounter was strange, like running into a past lover with your new one.

We wrote each other notes and always caught up after the weekends. I loved laughing at Gabriella's jokes. We took driver's education classes together. We also tried to study for tests together, but it usually resulted in a nap for me.

I soon added another best friend to my life, and everything happily chugged along until we graduated from high school.

Scarlett: University

Things grow complex when you leave the bubble of high school. No longer is the foundation for your friendship a shared school, schedule, and contempt for the subjects of Math and Geography. You need to make an effort to stay in touch as your lives change, especially if your ambitions take you out of the city you were raised in. That was definitely the case for me.

Looking back, I can see that my friendships ebbed and flowed. In my first year of university, I was closer to Gabriella, but in my last year, Scarlett and I spent more time together and kept in touch more often. After I graduated, I moved to another city to start a new job. I continued to change cities and jobs for a few years after that. Scarlett and I still kept in touch and visited each other.

But when she became engaged, deep down (without acknowledging this to myself), I became insecure and worried about the stability she and I had in our close friendship. I felt less needed, less vital; the time she had to spend with me was now shared with her fiancé and his friends. I thought that the comfort and security of our closeness were disappearing.

Valerie: My Mid-Twenties

Sometimes there is a specific moment that cements a friendship. My relationship with Valerie was like that. One night, when visiting my parents, I received a text message. "Do you want to meet up for a drink?" Valerie, whom I hadn't seen since the previous year, had messaged me out of the blue. It turned out that she was staying near my parents' place at a hotel. I happily accepted her invitation and drove to the hotel with a bottle of champagne for our catch-up, but I was met with sobs and revelations. My friend broke off her engagement a month before her wedding. She shared her thoughts, fears, and crushing guilt, and I comforted her. After that, she texted me every morning, and we talked day and night. She visited me in my new city, and I visited her in her hometown. We started making plans to go to Europe together the following summer.

My fears and anxieties about Scarlett getting married, and my life not having the same kind of momentum, subsided. Through my friendship with Valerie, I felt the comfort, safety, and security of having someone who needed me, made future plans with me, and wanted me around as much as possible. I was also able to lean on her in a way that my boyfriend and I didn't lean on each other. He and I both strived for independence from our relationship to feel secure. And here it was, the safety and security I wanted in the form of a new best friend.

I moved back to my new city a couple of years later and broke up with my long-term boyfriend. I plunged back into singlehood and navigated the brave new world of dating applications with Valerie at my side. Valerie and I both lived downtown, and we saw each other at least once or twice a week. We started exercise programs, discussed goals and dreams, and dissected our dating lives. We had many drinks on our balconies and enjoyed lazy Sundays together. We travelled together once a year and attended music festivals with our friends. The kind of closeness we had, well, it could only be compared to a long-term couple.

So why was I surprised when it turned out that there wasn't much room for me when my friend entered a serious relationship? No more dating and dabbling—this one became serious.

Valerie planned trips with her boyfriend, spent weekends at concerts with his friends, and enjoyed lazy Sundays at his place a town away. And even though I was in a serious relationship then, things were not going well. A couple of months before my best friend took the big step of moving in with her boyfriend a town away, my boyfriend and I broke up.

In that same period, I lost my job. Suddenly, less than a month after I turned 30, my life came crashing around me, and I didn't have the steady friendship support I'd had for the past five years. I felt abandoned and blamed Valerie for not being there for me and not including me in her plans now that she was coupled and I was single. But the reality was that she could no longer meet the expectations of our incredibly close relationship because she was building a new and different close relationship.

The year after I turned 30 brought many questions to light, and the one most significant among them: Are best friends really forever?

I learned a lot in that year and the few that followed. And I think I've managed to answer those questions. So here it goes—here's everything I learned the hard way.

Are Best Friends Really Forever?

When we give someone a title like Significant Other, Boyfriend, Partner, Best Friend, or Spouse, we have tied a set of expectations to that person. We have given them a role in our lives that we expect to remain steady. In the case of a spouse by marriage, that role is bound and defined by law. And we also usually take much care to outline the rules and expectations for our spouse, whether through vows or intimate conversations. We expect the relationship to remain pretty steady even as our lives change.

But the nature of friendships is that they are bound to change. We can't expect to always live in the same city, receive the same number of check-in texts or phone calls, plan the same number of trips every year, wear the same relationship status, and even maintain the same interests.

But sometimes, without realizing it, we name someone our best friend because we are trying to secure the friendship and the role that person plays in our life. We are trying to solidify this person's role and ensure it never changes. But the problem is that it most definitely will. If we can expect and anticipate that, we can more easily adapt to changes and allow that person's role to be flexible yet constant. When we don't expect change, we frustrate ourselves by thinking that everything should be able to stay the same, and we might start to resent the other person for the fact that the friendship is changing.

To maintain a best friendship or any other friendship, we have to flow with change. This means we stay clear on our desire and commitment to be friends but flexible on what that looks like, especially as our lives change over time. This is why communication is so important in relationships—as our lives change, we need to be able to work with the other person to meet their needs, our needs, and come to an agreement about how to fulfill those needs as the parameters of our lives change.

Emilia

If I had anticipated that change would be natural and necessary in my friendships, I would have more easily weathered the changes. I would have expected the fact that my closest friend or I might move to another city, even though we swore up and down that this would never be the case. Such is the nature of life—things change. Sometimes it's a job that necessitates a move, and sometimes it's a significant relationship. Or maybe someone has to move to take care of a family member. We can't expect our friendships to stay the same as the changes in our lives occur.

But what we can do is be honest. We can get creative about how to meet each other's needs. There are many ways to stay in touch and continue friendships even at a distance. It's all about finding ways that work for each friendship and being honest when we need more contact, face time, or phone calls. But as we honestly share our needs, we need to find a middle ground in our dialogue so our friends can openly share theirs.

So back to the question: Are best friends really forever?

Answer: *They can be if we are prepared to fight for them through the changing seasons of our lives.*

Key Learning

- Change is inevitable in every friendship.
- What we want in and from our friendships will change as we age.
- We have to be honest with our friends and find compromises if we want to navigate change successfully.

Discussion Questions

1. Do you have a best friend?
2. If so, how has your friendship changed over time?
3. Have you successfully adapted to the changing landscape of your friendship?

Friendship Expectations

"You have no expectations of me. You are very grateful and content with my friendship and what I have to offer."

Fervent declarations of undying devotion that only death can sever are pledged before witnesses when people marry. Smart business partners typically adhere to a legally binding agreement relating to roles and expectations. Nevertheless, few are the friends who signed any documents of fidelity or discussed expectations at the outset of their friendships. Of the 110 women who responded to the survey, when asked if they discussed expectations of each other for their female friendships, less than 25% did. Yet, we all carry expectations about what a friend should or should not do for us. Can we expect our friends to meet our needs if we don't let them know what these needs are?

Our lives are ever-changing, and inevitably, our needs will change depending on the situation. Is it fair for us to expect that our friends anticipate our changing needs and conform to our rigid expectations? What happens if an unvoiced expectation goes unmet? If we don't tell our friends what we want from the beginning, what are the chances that we will later voice our concerns? And if we do, will it leave our friends blind-sided?

At the most basic level, we expect our close friends to care about us and demonstrate this by keeping in touch, sharing about themselves, supporting us, and accepting us without judgement. That's a given, right? A good friend should do these things. And duh, we shouldn't have to tell them to. A good friend should just know.

Yet, when our most basic expectations are not met, we feel unloved and unappreciated.

Determining Our Expectations

Identifying and understanding the underlying expectations we have of our friends is essential. One way to do this is to consider a previous conflict with your friend. What happened that made you upset? Which unconscious "friendship rule" was broken? Reflection will allow us to create a list of truths (or beliefs) about what friendship means to us and the subsequent expectations that branch out from those beliefs. Whether we share this list with our friends or have it for reference, it will serve as a checkpoint when things get rocky. It will also give us a chance to examine the viability of our expectations. However, before we get to the documentation of our expectations, let's look at this illustration:

> When Sou-Yen's partner was hospitalized due to a life-threatening illness, she called her friend Chloe immediately. She felt extremely overwhelmed and expected Chloe to drop everything to be with her. It's what she, Sou-Yen, would have done. But Chloe didn't come immediately or soon after that (though she called that evening). Sou-Yen was very upset. Did she tell Chloe? No, she never discussed it.

Keep this story in mind. We will be referencing it again as we delve further into this topic of expectations.

Let's turn our attention to your expectations of your female friends. Be as specific as possible so that if you had to share it with someone, your meaning would be very clear.

1. Consider some conflicts you've had with friends in the past or recently. Which belief about friendship did these behaviours threaten?

2. Give thought to the things that would be very hard to 'swallow' if your friend did them to you.

3. As you consider the first two questions, write down as many beliefs about friendships that these situations (imaginary or real) highlight for you.

4. Make a list of all the qualities and attributes you want in a friend due to your beliefs about friendship.

5. How flexible are your expectations for your friendships? Under what circumstances do you think it would be ok to break your friendship rules?

6. Include the activities and events (as many as you can think of) that you expect your friend to involve you in and vice versa.

7. Now, review your list. Clarify anything unclear and add anything that's missing.

8. Next, place an asterisk beside the most critical items to any friendships you have (If you have more than 10 items starred, whittle it down to your top 10).

Below is an example of a list. Yours might look different or have additional items.

Top 10 Female Friendship Expectations (Sample):

1. Communicate with me at least once per week by direct messaging.
2. Spend face-to-face time with me at least once per month to talk and share without distractions (video calls are fine if face-to-face get-togethers are not possible).
3. Include me in her personal activities and events.
4. Include me in her family activities and events.
5. Have integrity—must be honest and ethical.
6. Listen and support me emotionally when I need it.
7. Show or tell me how important I am to her.
8. Hold me accountable and call me out on situations when I get down on myself.
9. Must be kind, considerate, and thoughtful toward me and others.
10. Be my cheerleader and a vital part of my support system.

Reviewing your list, can you think of a friend, old or new, who meets or exceeds your listed expectations? Does she possess other qualities you did not even know you would enjoy having in a friend? (Add these to your list and refine it, if needed).

Friends who possess these key attributes are the friendships you want to hang on to and fight for. For those not fulfilling even a third of the items on your list of expectations, consider why you might be hanging on to this friendship (See Chapter 7: Breaking Up, pg. 77).

Discussing Our Expectations: When, How, and Why

At which point in the friendship is it safe or advisable to discuss our expectations? At the outset? At a defining moment? When hashing through a conflict? First of all, it's not in anyone's best interest to raise issues where none previously existed. If your current friendships are already rock solid and you are content with your relationship, just affirm them. However, if you've been suffering in silence over the years because of repeated slights or irritants perpetrated by your friend, for your peace of mind and continued mental wellness, it's time to sound the alarm.

Typically, the best time to address an issue is soon after the incident. At the time of the incident, we might be too upset or emotionally compromised to express ourselves adequately. Here is one approach:

Example I:

1. Schedule a meet-up with your friend at a suitable time and venue.
2. Outline the incident that took place.
3. Explain how her behaviour during that incident made you feel (without blaming her).
4. Remind her how much you value her friendship and the other wonderful attributes she has.
5. Let her know what you'd like her to do differently in the future.
6. Address any questions or clarifications resulting from your disclosure.
7. Affirm her for hearing you out.
8. Close the topic and enjoy the rest of your time together.

Another approach for a long-standing, unaddressed issue might be to use your newly crafted Friendship Expectations List.

Example II:

1. You could invite your friend(s) to make a similar list at your next meet-up or purely as an exercise in relationship enrichment.
2. Share how many items on your list are provided by that friend and thank her for those (what friend would not love to receive such words of affirmation!).
3. Pick one thing you'd like her to do more or less (especially if it has been an ongoing irritant).
4. Talk about it using an approach similar to Example I. Remember, it's never too late to share what you need and expect from your friends. Just do it with tact.

But… it feels uncomfortable.

What if the very thought of spelling out your expectations to your friend(s) leaves you feeling squeamish? Some things should be fought for and hashed out in a friendship despite how difficult or uncomfortable the conversation might be. If a friend is using you, persistently putting you down, or excluding you, you should call them out on the behaviour, although we do have to pick our battles. We first need to assess what we receive from the relationship against what we don't have. If we later compare the balance sheet and determine that the good outweighs the bad, or the positives are more significant than the negatives, we should let the 'irritant' go and make peace with what remains.

The Percentages Are Not Always Equal

Our friendships will not always be 50/50. Sometimes we have to cut our friends a bit of slack when circumstances or situations prevent them from being there for us as much as possible. What we want to end up with is a friendship where we feel valued, loved, respected, and appreciated–if not all the time, then most of the time.

Let's return to Sou-Yen and Chloe. In later reflection on how upset she was about Chloe's 'lack of support,' Sou-Yen realized she was so focused on her needs that she did not consider Chloe's situation. As a recently divorced single mother not receiving any financial support from her ex, Chloe prioritized her job to provide for her young family. She couldn't afford to drop everything to come to Sou-Yen's aid without jeopardizing her livelihood. Sou-Yen also learned later on that Chloe does not like to be in intensely stressful situations (like Sou-Yen's partner's fight for his life).

Whose needs take priority in these situations?

To complicate matters, Sou-Yen did not know that she would need, let alone expect, that specific type of support from her friend Chloe until that incident. Therefore, even when we make a list of expectations and check it twice, newly discovered expectations can surprise us. In processing her expectation of Chloe, Sou-Yen learned that aside from the job issue, Chloe would not be a great support to her in those situations. So, Sou-Yen had to face a moment of truth: that type of support would never be realized from her friend Chloe.

So, what do we do when we come to these moments of realization? Sever the relationship? Not necessarily. In this case, Sou-Yen dialed back her expectations. What remained was still enough to continue her friendship with Chloe once she adjusted her expectations.

If you recall, Sou-Yen never discussed how she felt with Chloe. One could argue that she should have allowed Chloe to hear how she felt; withholding how her lack of support made Sou-Yen feel implies that she does not trust Chloe to be honest with her. Maybe.

The fact of the matter is that Sou-Yen was uncomfortable with having this discussion. It felt too confrontational and needy. She was uncomfortable asking for this emotional support, even though she wanted and needed it. She wanted it to be given freely and unprompted. Unfortunately, the stark reality is that Chloe can never deliver what she needs in this area. To bring it up would introduce a degree of awkwardness into the relationship that is not worth it.

But what about unmet expectations?

If our friends genuinely care for us, shouldn't they do everything to ensure we feel their love and commitment once we share our expectations? That might be what we desire or hope for, but the reality is that our friends cannot give us everything we expect them to, even when we tell them what we want. It might not be within their area of competence or comfort zone.

Expectations of Reciprocal Investment

Some things should be a requirement of all mature friendships. One of these things is the expectation of reciprocal (not necessarily equal) investment of the other person in the friendship. What if we find that the friendship pendulum is perpetually on the side of us contributing more than the other person to the relationship? Are we going to discuss the issue or not?

Based on our survey, 54% of 110 women who answered this question would invest less or pull back if they were contributing more to the relationship. Only 19% said they would discuss it head-on. Could it be that in female-to-female friendships, many of us assume that our friends should want to be with us as much as we want to be with them? And when they don't comply, we feel we have no right to demand to know why or request accountability?

Pregya loves to keep connected with her friends, so she will reach out when she hasn't heard from them for a month or so. One friend in particular (let's call her Mari) would always respond to her call with the line: "I was just thinking of calling you." Every time Pregya would call, she'd get the same response. Following one such check-in time, Pregya told Mari that she'd wait to hear from her next time since it seemed she was always pre-empting her call.

After about two and a half months of not hearing from her friend, Pregya called Mari and asked about her lack of contact. Mari profusely apologized. Life was busy (work, children, etc.). However, this time, Pregya told Mari that her lack of investment in the friendship made her feel like she was not important. She also told Mari that this would be the last call she would initiate. Again, Mari promised to do better but never did. The relationship died—not from acrimony but a lack of reciprocity.

In the above illustration, Pregya decided, following a long period of Mari making concessions for her busy life and Pregya hoping she would do better, to discuss the issue head-on. She voiced her expectations and asked for what she needed. Unfortunately, sharing or discussing our expectations does not always guarantee a happily ever after. When Pregya's voiced expectation did not change Mari's behaviour, she pulled back, and the friendship died. She was the only one keeping it together.

It is not a healthy, satisfying friendship when one person is left experiencing a lack of reciprocal commitment. The expectation of reciprocal investment is one of those areas that, if left unaddressed, is highly frustrating to the soul of the one who is always reaching out.

A Word About Neglect

When we find ourselves more invested in the friendship than the other person and discover we do not matter to them as much as they matter to us, we begin to experience the effects of neglect. We receive little or no nurturing, appreciation, or affirmation and feel taken advantage of and excluded.

Prolonged neglect must not be something we settle for in our friendships. When we start feeling neglected by our close friends, we should not shy away from addressing the issue comprehensively. Griping to someone else about how rattily the friend is treating us or silently stewing about the neglect makes for a miserable existence.

Companionship, intimacy, and kinship all help us thrive. It should be a basic expectation of all our friendships that they do not neglect us for too long.

Realistic vs. Unrealistic Expectations

A friend might expect you to be the Godparent of her child, fetch her dry-cleaning because it's on your way home, drop and run to the rescue whenever she calls, and expect you to be present at every birthday and life event. Unfortunately, you may not learn about these expectations until you're 'broadsided' by them.

Expectations are not a set of demands. Telling your friend that you expect her to show up at your child's birthday party every year with an expensive gift and a food item is a demand. What if she can't afford expensive gifts? What if she cannot attend the party one year in particular? Is the friendship over?

Ellie and Olivia had been friends since childhood. They remained close and fully participated in each other's lives through the years. When Olivia's boyfriend asked her to marry him, Ellie was elated for her friend and looked forward to sharing the excitement of the wedding planning. Soon after, however, Olivia started to ask things of Ellie that caught her unawares. Olivia expected her to organize multiple wedding showers with various friend and family groups and attend at least three formal bridesmaids' galas—two of which were out of town and required plane tickets and expensive outfits, in addition to the bridesmaid dress she would be paying for—and a whole lot more. It got to be too much.

When Ellie complained to Olivia, she was told that, as a friend, she should do what makes the bride happy. Things got increasingly awkward from then on, and the wedding day was no exception. One friend participated resentfully, and the other was incapable of understanding the perceived lack of support.

Whether Olivia's expectations were realistic is not the issue. Ideally, she should have checked in with Ellie to see if she was okay with everything she asked her to do. When she found out that Ellie struggled to cater to her expectations, one would think she would consider Ellie's feelings. Instead, she insisted on what she wanted to the detriment of her friend.

This is another example of unknown expectations. It is possible that Olivia did not know that she was behaving like a Bridezilla. Even if she did not have this expectation on her list, it was somewhere in her mind, waiting for the right occasion to manifest itself. That tells us that we should be prepared for whacky or situational expectations in our friendship journeys. True friends will ensure that they are not putting a treasured friend in an uncomfortable position in fulfilling their needs. Our love for our friends propels us to seek their good.

Takers and Givers

Before we part from the topic of expectations, let's briefly talk about Takers and Givers. A Giver-Taker friendship occurs when one friend is focused on catering to their friend's needs (the Giver), and the other (the Taker) is focused on their own needs and what they're getting from the friendship. If both parties are happy with their roles, the mutual needs of the friendship are met.

Problems occur, however, when a Giver expects the Taker to give as much as she does. Entrenched Takers will resist this expectation even when pointed out to her. Rare are the instances where a Taker wants the Giver to take (unless she is setting things up for a bigger payoff). The Taker will take as long as the Giver is willing to give and may even punish the Giver when she's not giving enough, not giving frequently, or giving the desired type of gifts.

Key Learning

- Expectations are not a set of demands.
- Identifying and sharing our friendship expectations will help keep our friendships healthy.
- Some expectations are non-negotiable and should be fought for even if it makes us uncomfortable.
- Timing and approach are important when discussing unrealistic or unmet expectations.
- Discussing expectations can provide opportunities to affirm our friends.
- Be understanding when life circumstances impact our friends' ability to support us as they used to.

Discussion Questions

1. At which point during a friendship is it appropriate to talk about expectations?
2. How do you address unrealistic expectations from your friends?
3. What have you learned about yourself from your list of friendship expectations?
4. What's one wish you just haven't been able to receive from current or past female friendships?

Friendship Roles

"My actions have always been louder than my words. Love is an action word. I choose you every time."

When we asked our survey respondents to select the primary roles they take on in their female friendships, Supporter/Cheerleader (87%) was the clear frontrunner. When we asked our respondents to say what they see as the benefits of female friendships, words like 'support' and 'understanding' were repeated frequently:

- They are supportive and stick with you through thick and thin.
- They support you during the good and bad times, no matter what.
- Having someone to talk to about my feelings and experiences and receiving emotional support.
- Mutual understanding.
- Understanding on a variety of levels.
- Someone who cares.
- Feelings of acceptance, mutual respect, and understanding.

Good friends support each other emotionally. Good friends try to understand what you're feeling. Good friends respect one another. That's not all they can do, but we are in a good place when we have those elements in our friendships.

With that as a backdrop, this chapter will focus on the other roles we play in our female friendships—those we chose, those assigned to us, or those inherited by default (because no one else wanted them)—as well as how to have that difficult conversation when these roles become problematic.

The Roles We Play

Over and above the factors that initially drew us to each other and kept us invested in our friendships, there is an underlying system that runs the friendship engine effectively. Like the varied roles needed to run a train, from conductor to engineer, we each contribute an important and necessary function to our friendship with our roles. We may or may not play the same role in all our friend groups, but we all take on roles beyond being supportive, respectful, and understanding. Roles are necessary to make the friend 'ship' run smoothly. But how did we get into these roles? Did we pick them, or were they assigned to us?

> Kenya is part of a triad of friends who've known each other since high school. They set aside the week leading up to the Labour Day weekend every year. Significant others are told upfront about this 'sacred' time for 'the sistahs,' as they call themselves. Kenya's friends, Marissa and Avery, describe her as very particular. Kenya has high standards for everything: where they will stay, the level of service required, and cleaning practices. Because of her fastidiousness, Marissa and Avery have, over time, found that it's better and less fractious to let Kenya be the booking agent for their annual meetups.

This is a clear example of how Kenya's 'fastidiousness' (a personality trait) determined a particular friendship role. The above example illustrates that who we are and what we desire can create a specific dynamic in our female friendships. Remember those group projects from high school or college? The teacher would pre-assign group members for special projects to show us how to work in teams (or torture us). If we were lucky, we would end up with a group where each member contributed equally in time and content. If we were unlucky, we would invariably end up in a group with that one person who never shows up for meetings and never does the work assigned but fully expects to benefit from the team's efforts.

How Do We Get into the Roles We Play?

Think of our friendships as groups or teams (dyads or more). As Kenya's illustration shows, she took on a role (booking agent) that helped her meet a personal need due to her personality. The one who likes to take control will likely take on the organizer role in her friendship. The one who loves to receive affirmation will initiate conversations that provide that type of exchange when she gets together with her friends. And the one who enjoys being pampered will likely do things to pamper her friends and may react poorly when her friend(s) do not reciprocate. These are examples of how our personality and preferences might lead us to behave in specific ways and expect certain things in the context of our friendships.

Then, there are the roles we did not wish for but have been 'forced' to play because (1) nobody else wanted the role, or (2) we were co-opted into it. This dynamic plays out mostly in friendship groups (though dyads have been known to experience this type of role assignment by the dominant member of the dyad). This type of role assignment can have its origin in a simple situation.

For example, a group of friends have a sleepover at one of their homes. Everyone feels pretty relaxed, and the conversation eventually leads to what to do for dinner. Options are considered and discarded until the group decides to eat in and have the meal delivered. No one, however, is making a move to place the order. Finally, someone (the hungriest or the most impatient with the process) steps up and volunteers to order the meal. However, since the time that successfully executed order and delicious meal took place, the group has come to rely on and expect the friend to perform this duty every time. This volunteer, who never wanted this role in the first place and hoped that the next time, out of fairness, someone else would take it on, grows increasingly resentful.

How might she discuss this 'inequity' with her friends? What if she has tried, but the friends 'pooh-poohed' her angst—telling her she's good at it, so she should keep doing it? Or what if they promise to do better, but they never do, so she feels obligated (because it's not that big of a deal to order a meal) to keep doing it.

The point is that even in a supportive friendship group, a member can still experience a lack of understanding, reciprocity, or in the above case, feel a lack of respect for her position on an issue. Over time, this resentment can eat away at all the good things in the friendship if left unaddressed.

Or consider these other scenarios: What if either Marissa or Avery (Kenya's friends) are interested in the role of booking agent? What if Kenya has grown tired of her role? What if Kenya is fine with her role but is internally stewing because Marissa never has her money ready when it is needed, or that Avery always finds something about the venue to complain about? What if Kenya feels unappreciated for her effort to make sure the accommodations are perfect for them all to enjoy? How do these friends communicate feelings about or re-negotiate roles that have kept the friendship engine running smoothly?

Dr. Murray Bowen[2], a psychiatrist, purports that families function as an 'emotional' interconnected system. This interconnection is necessary because it helps the family protect, care for, and support each other. What each member does impacts the others in the unit. In other words, any change in one member's functioning affects the unit's foundational structure. When a member cannot 'play' their proper role in the family unit, it triggers an alarm, forcing the system to adjust to the threat. Suppose the malfunctioning member cannot return to their role? In that case, another family member will have to step into that role (while balancing their current role) so the family system can keep functioning effectively.

Dysfunctional family systems operate in the same way. They need someone to be 'sick' for it to run. When the 'sick' person seeks help and starts to heal, this also triggers an alarm within the entire unit, which will try to either return the member to sickness or force someone else into that role.

Similar dynamics may play out, especially in close-knit friendship groups. We each need the other to do something, be something, or allow us to be a particular way to feel safe and healthy. When that need is not met, we may resort to behaviours that will force our friends' hands, so to speak, or leave the friendship to get that need met elsewhere. Therefore, open and honest communication is necessary to keep our friendships robust and dynamic. Dynamic because any system that cannot adjust to the changing needs and times runs the risk of becoming irrelevant, obsolete, or unfairly rigid.

[2] The Bowen Center for the Study of the Family. http://www.thebowencenter.org/

What Happens When We Want to Change Our Roles?

Yvonne

I have two different pockets of close friends. One is a triad and the other a quad. Within the triad, each person seems to monitor each other's contributions from an operational point of view. If one person pays for lunch, the other will do so the next time. If one person is doing the organizing, the others either ask how she can assist, or together they pre-determine what each person will do. We meet regularly to discuss new developments and monitor things along the way. So, from an operational point of view, when a project is in the works, each person takes on a role needed to bring the project to fruition.

My project role does not change my personality and how it plays out in my friendship. I will always be the one to initiate conversations around personal growth and development or get us to talk about our struggles and affirm each other. Another friend is a great listener and an effective sounding board for ideas. She prefers to support her more outgoing friends from backstage. She is reliable and trustworthy. The other friend is the dominant leader, restless and active; she is always ready to take us on the next adventure. This group works for me because, individually and together, we care for each other and work very hard to be fair and accommodating.

My quad group has different dynamics at play. I had a friendship with each woman previously, and now jointly, we have a long history of spending time together. We talk, we joke, we expound, and we poke fun. We are spiritual, irreverent, vulnerable, strong, independent, and full of humour. When we get together, time flies by quickly. We are usually the last to leave a restaurant as tired wait staff impatiently usher us out the door to our profound apologies and giggles. These women are my rock. We don't get together often. We don't talk every week. But we each know that we've got each other's backs when things turn sour in our lives. In this group, I am still the same me that likes to affirm people and make sure we affirm each other. Each of us brings something different to the relationship.

Yet, as much as I love and respect these groups of women and others who are my rock-solid friends, I am reluctant to raise issues that might lead to awkwardness in our relationship. If it's important or causing me enough grief, I will, but I have to work myself up. At one of our last meetings of the quad group, one of the friends complained that we had not gone on a vacation for a while. Internally I rolled my eyeballs. This is, for me, an ongoing bone of contention. We had not gone on a holiday because I had not organized it – a role I took on for a long while and had informed them on multiple occasions that I no longer wished to be solely responsible for. At the end of our last vacation, as everyone was waxing eloquently on how good it was to spend time together and how we should do it more often, I had stated in clear, specific terms that someone else would have to take on the coordination role. To date, no one has.

So, what will I do about it, especially when I know that they will continue, if I let them, to default to me on this one thing? Is it worth walking away from the friendship?

Our friends are not perfect. They will not always rise to the occasion and behave reasonably. But my love for my friends and theirs for me overshadow our shortcomings. I know I have their support and loyalty. Our communication may not be as frequent as I wish, but our shared history, the mutual respect we have for each other, and the kindness and compassion I have experienced from these women trump my desires that they may never fulfill. When I examine my heart, I find I'm okay with that. The benefits far outweigh the annoyances. And as I think about what I may never get from them, I wonder what they might need that they never tell me.

Conversations About Role Fatigue

You have to evaluate if a role issue in your friendship is bothering you enough to warrant a discussion. If you think you'll implode if you have to perform in this role ad infinitum, you need to talk with your friend(s). If the love and support are genuine and respect is there, then have it out. However, in all difficult friendship conversations, timing is everything, so choose a good time and see if these recommended steps help you achieve your desired outcome (See Chapter 5, Friendship Conflict, pg. 45). Here is a potential approach to the conversation:

1. Once you meet and everyone is ready to talk, affirm your friend(s) for the value they bring into your life.
2. Explain the reason for your meeting.
3. Describe (without going on forever and being accusatory) how you feel about your role and what you'd like to do differently.
4. Give your friend(s) time to ask questions or seek clarification.
5. Affirm again all that you love about the friendship.
6. Agree (or if the person needs time to digest, ask how much time they need) on a new course of action.

Addressing the Power Dynamics in Your Friendship Gr oup

Not all friendships are egalitarian. Power dynamics play out in many friendship groups. The group leader (the one deferred to for decision-making) knowingly or unknowingly controls the agenda. This is particularly evident in friendship groups that have a childhood history. The group will do fine if the leader is benevolent and does not take undue advantage of her privilege. Where we run into problems is when the group leader abuses her position. For example, she only supports those activities and projects that she likes, she does not recognize the value in her friends outside of making her happy, or others feel intimidated talking about what they need from the friendship.

It can be hard to raise issues you have tolerated for many years. The friend may ask why you haven't said anything all this time. What will you answer? Why are you raising the issue now? Are you stronger, tired, or completely fed up? Know your reasons so you can explain them.

1. Identify a specific behaviour by the friend and how it makes you feel.
2. Be prepared for resistance.
3. Be prepared for adverse consequences. This can take the form of silencing, exclusion, loss of the friendship, the perks that come with it, and the support of others who might be pressured to take sides with her against you.

Remember that a friendship where you are not valued and respected is not a good friendship. You deserve better.

Key Learning

- Good friends respect and support each other.
- Some friendship roles are chosen, and some are assigned.
- The roles we take on in our friendships say a lot about what we need from the friendship.
- Family systems dynamics can also play out in friendship relationships.
- Role fatigue happens.
- Conversations regarding changes to friendship roles require thought and planning.
- Power dynamics can play out in both dyadic and group friendships.

Discussion Questions

1. How comfortable would you feel discussing changes to roles in your friendship group or dyad?
2. Who, if anyone, would you say has the power in your friendship group? What do they have power or control over?
3. What accounts for our hesitation to raise issues around the dynamics in our friendships?

Friendship Conflict

"Hurt people hurt people. We all have things about us that may annoy each other; we all behave within our capacity. Some can't be everything you need."

At an event for a couple celebrating many years of marriage, the wife commented that one of the things that kept them together for so long was their difference of opinions. She said, "If both of us behave, think, and act exactly the same, then one of us is redundant."

When we have differences of opinions or dissimilarities in approach to issues, in the very act of coexisting with the people in our lives, we will occasionally rub each other the wrong way. Our female friendships are no exception. Despite the love and regard for each other, we are still distinct people with our own opinions, behaviours, and habits. Sometimes we will experience conflict.

Causes of Conflict

What causes conflict? What things get you bent out of shape in your female friendships?

Yvonne

I have a close friend that I've known for many years who, over time, has become a bit of a conspiracy theorist. She attributes many things that have a logical explanation to the government and people in power trying to control the "small" people. One day, as she was espousing her ideologies and I was equally engaged in presenting 'logical' counterarguments, the thought entered my mind, "How did I end up being this person's friend? I so completely disagree with her stance!" On the heels of that thought, I pictured my life without her and immediately stopped arguing. That is the package that comes with who she is. We take the good and the not-so-good, and on the balance sheet of my mind, the good outweighed the bad. Nowadays, I listen to her spout her philosophies but do not engage. It is an argument I will never win and is not worth the headache.

Any small or large thing can cause conflict given the right circumstances. Here are some typical examples:

- Too much time together in close quarters
- Differences of opinions
- Perceived or intended slights
- Unmet expectations
- Exclusions
- Betrayal
- Hurt feelings
- Tiredness
- Bottled-up emotions

And what is it that our respondents get into conflict over? Women who responded to this question in our survey cited the following examples:

- Being berated in public
- Keeping shared space messy
- Not spending enough time on the relationship
- Dislike of friend's partner
- Reaction to a family situation
- Cheating
- Ghosting
- Lying
- Feeling judged
- Differences of opinions
- Undercutting
- Asking for advice and not taking it
- Different parenting styles
- Different views of morality
- Misrepresentation

Whatever the cause or underlying reason for the conflict, once it hits the relationship fan, it is a problem that, if left unaddressed, can fester and negatively impact the relationship.

How We Tend to Deal with Conflict

How we perceive and deal with conflict is learned.

Yvonne

For me, any kind of passionate shouting from angry-looking faces means a big, nasty showdown is about to occur where people could get hurt. As soon as I hear the shouting, my radar immediately goes to high alert—get out! I learned this firsthand from observing conflict with my parental figures as a child. As I got older and more exposed to other families, I discovered that not all passionate shouting signifies impending violence. However, I still prefer quiet, reasoned resolution to problems. Once the yelling starts, I feel the urge to run.

And it is not just the yelling that cramps my stomach. Someone being angry with me, shutting me out, or unjustly accusing me of something produces similar reactions. Conflicts make me uncomfortable, tense, and anxious. It robs me of sleep and pre-occupies my mind until a resolution is reached. So, how does this impact my female friendships?

Given my internalized relationship with conflict, I try, within my power, to avoid them or address issues before they become full-blown and uncontrollable. Over time, I have learned that sometimes one must stand up and fight instead of running. So, when the issue is significant, I choose to fight for what I want, even though it is something I need to gear up for emotionally. In these cases, I have determined that cowering, running, or avoiding is not conducive to my growth and mental well-being.

I cannot recall any significant conflicts with my cluster of female friends. That said, if I believe a friendship is not good for me or a friend is not amenable to investing in the relationship, I gradually reduce contact and communication until the friendship fizzles.

Emilia

Like Yvonne, I have an internalized relationship with conflict that can make it tough to address issues head-on. Some of my friendships—especially in the second half of my 20s—have increased my comfort level with direct, solution-oriented conflict. I am definitely more capable than I used to be in this respect, but I still struggle with some friendships that tend to gloss over issues or avoid potential contentions.

Beyond my perspective, women can sometimes have a more difficult time being honest when something is troubling them in their friendship with another female. Perhaps this is because we expect other women to understand us, and we are flummoxed when they don't. Unlike our relationships and friendships with men, we assume similarities breed understanding.

This showed up in the results of our questionnaire. Based on our 110 respondents, women tend to deal with conflict in the following ways:

1. **Think things through, then address:** 54% of our respondents indicate that when conflict arises with friends, they take time to think things through and then address it. Some like to discuss the issue with another friend or partner to get a different perspective on the situation. We can't always count on our emotional barometer to give us a proper perspective when conflicts arise, so getting another trusted perspective on the issue is a great way to deal with things. We consider this the best approach because emotions will have time to settle, and a thoughtful approach, sensitive to our friends' feelings, can be applied.

2. **Ruminate but don't act:** 15% of our respondents say they ruminate but do not act. Should every perceived or real slight done to us by our friends be addressed? We certainly

don't think so. No one is perfect, and we can definitely chalk up some actions or words to each person's unique points of view. Some people are also more sensitive than others. Others tend to see slights where none were intended. The more self-aware we are, the better we can determine if a situation warrants a confrontation. Not everything is worth fighting over. We can elect to cut our friends and ourselves a bit of slack.

That said, if the situation or incident has happened before and leaves you feeling disrespected or hurt, then you should address it. Ruminating without acting is not likely going to resolve the conflict. It is akin to putting one's head in the sand and hoping things will blow over with time. Instead, it can be helpful to put your thoughts in writing to help you clarify the situation and your feelings. Once you are happy with what you've written, you can send it to your friend if a face-to-face discussion fazes you.

If you decide to send the letter, make sure you are sensitive to your friend's feelings. Do not write things in anger that you might want to take back later. Taking the time to thoughtfully put your feelings into words can offer you and your friend time to digest and respond to what you have to say.

3. **Address immediately and directly:** Only 14% of our respondents said they had used this approach. Addressing issues immediately and directly requires clarity of thought, control of one's emotions, and respect for others. When we react in the moment, the issue is addressed, but damage can be done to our friend's feelings when this approach isn't taken with respect and care. For example, let's say your friend berated you publicly for showing up late for an event. Yes, you were late. Yes, you understand that she does not like to be kept waiting. But traffic was terrible, or maybe

public transit was slow. Your friend's direct approach was very public and embarrassed you thoroughly. It left you with a bad feeling that made you less likely to want to make plans with this friend again. This is an example of how the direct approach addressed the issue but damaged the friendship.

Use the direct and immediate approach when there is a clear violation of your rights and when you have the opportunity to speak to the person 'off-camera' (privately). If not, sit on it until an appropriate time (not too long, though). This will give you both perspective and ease in addressing the issue with your friend candidly, clearly, and respectfully.

Again, how each of us deals with conflict is learned. Reflect on how conflict was dealt with in your home when you were a child. This will give clues on how you might currently deal with conflict. Once you are aware of your relationship with conflict, it will help you gain insight and provide a starting point to learning healthy ways of dealing with it if, like us, you associate it with emotional stress.

Is the Conflict Worthy of a Fight?

If we take on everything that annoys or stresses us, we will likely find our friendships in a perpetual state of turbulence. For this reason, it's a good idea to be mindful about what we choose to bring up or argue about with others, mainly because we don't all think the same way. What's problematic for one person might feel completely normal for another. For example, we might get annoyed because we just cleaned the sink, and immediately a friend puts a dirty cup in it instead of placing it in the dishwasher or taking a moment to hand-wash it. Or maybe during a weekend getaway, a girlfriend leaves the bathroom countertop messy, and we have to clean it up if we want to enjoy our morning routine. Or perhaps a co-worker keeps using the Kleenex on our desk instead of going to get her own box.

All of the above examples can be annoying. Each of us needs to decide for ourselves which of the annoyances in our relationships are worth fighting about. Some are. Some are not.

Yvonne

My roommate had a higher tolerance for dirty dishes in the sink than I did. In my world, dishes are washed soon after dinner, and if not, certainly before one goes to bed. Nothing sets my day on the wrong course more than being greeted by a dirty kitchen first thing in the morning. Many are the conversations I had with my friend. We created schedules. We planned that I would do the washing up four times per week, and she would do it three times. But often, she would forget. I spoke with her about it, and she told me to lighten up! But she did try. She would make an effort for a day or two, but her good intentions never lasted.

I tried waiting until all the dishes were dirty, thinking this would get her to see the error of her ways. But when she was hungry, she pulled a plate from the mound in the sink and used it. Sometimes she would wash the one item she needed and ignore the rest. My stress and annoyance level hovered at the explosion point. I became sullen and crabby to be around while my friend seemed perfectly content and living her best life.

I complained about her behaviour to an older, wiser female friend, who told me I had a choice. I could choose to be right and miserable or do what was necessary to preserve my happiness and mental health. It dawned on me that this was an issue I could fix by simply taking on the responsibility of dishwashing instead of watching and waiting for my friend to do it and getting upset when she didn't. A clean kitchen was important to me but not something that came naturally to her. Once I did that, my stress reduced, and I returned to being my more pleasant self.

Here's another example:

One morning, I went to my husband's den to ask him a question. He promptly replied by saying that he was not talking to me. Surprised, I asked why. He mentioned something I had said or done the day before that bugged him. Now, my husband is even more introverted than I am, so I had not clued in that his quietness meant he was angry with me. I probably should have been more sensitive, but I started to laugh. I asked, "What is the point of being angry with someone if they don't even know?" There I was, having a perfectly pleasant day, clueless and happy, while he was stewing the whole time. What a waste of a perfectly good stew! When I put it that way to him, he saw the absurdity of his approach and even chuckled at the situation. We talked about what had bothered him and immediately resolved the issue.

Lesson: *Stewing in silence does not make your friend's life miserable—just yours.*

What annoys me does not necessarily annoy you. As stated at the beginning of this chapter, we are all different people and not carbon copies of each other. We do things differently and pay attention to different things. If you find yourself in a constant state of low-grade anger because your friend repeatedly does something you find inconsiderate or annoying, it is a good idea to speak up. Airing our grievances does not guarantee a solution to the problem but staying silent does guarantee that the issue will likely reoccur.

In most solid friendships, if you address the issue with tact and within a reasonable period of time, your friend will likely want to resolve it with you. However, if you cannot come to a mutual solution, you might have to give some serious thought to the future of your friendship. Reflecting on this can help you put the issue into perspective and find a way forward or a boundary you can implement on your own.

Key Learning

- Conflict will arise in our relationships, even in our female friendships.
- We all deal with conflict in different ways.
- How we deal with conflict is learned in our early years.
- Many women are not comfortable handling conflict in their female friendships.
- We all think differently, and for this reason, communication is essential. Your friend might not realize they've done something to annoy you.
- Addressing conflict does not guarantee a solution but staying silent almost guarantees that the issue will come up again.

Discussion Questions

1. Is the absence of conflict in a friendship a sign of a healthy relationship?
2. What is your relationship with conflict?
3. What specific issue(s) tend to trigger a conflict for you?
4. Does addressing an issue guarantee that you will reach an acceptable resolution?
5. Have there been situations where, due to your sensitivity, you've misread or misinterpreted a friend's action as a slight? If yes, how did you deal with it?

Maintaining our Friendships

"The friends that reciprocate and are actively involved and interested in your life are the ones you should work hard at keeping"

We elaborated earlier on the importance of knowing our friendship expectations. We also made the case that our friends may not be able to meet all of our needs and expectations. Our 110 respondents have invested many years in their friendships, averaging approximately 25 years of friendship per person. What is the secret to maintaining a dynamic, flexible female friendship that will stand the test of time?

We all want to be supported, validated, and appreciated by our treasured female friends. Yet, despite our best intentions, we can hurt or upset the women in our lives that offer us these precious gifts. This can happen when we (1) take each other for granted, (2) neglect our friends, (3) become unintentionally self-absorbed, or (4) aren't aware of each other's love language.

Love Languages

In Gary Chapman's book, *The Five Love Languages*[3], he identified five ways through which married couples express and receive love. We believe that identifying and applying Chapman's love languages principles can also improve our female friendships. Chapman's five love languages are as follows:

1. **Words of affirmation:** I enjoy hearing (or reading) how someone feels about me directly.
2. **Acts of service:** I enjoy it when someone helps me with tasks or does something that lightens my load. For example, by offering to bring me food or medication when I am sick.
3. **Physical touch:** I enjoy hugs or linking arms, which allows me to physically feel you close to me.
4. **Quality time:** I appreciate it when you carve out time in your life for me.
5. **Giving gifts:** When you take the time to select and bring me gifts, large or small, it makes me feel important to you.

Learning what our friends need to feel genuinely appreciated might seem like a no-brainer. After all, many women have been friends for years and have weathered personal and relational storms without a course on love languages. However, the longevity of a relationship is not necessarily an indication of its health or our satisfaction with it. Neither is the frequency of communication. Many friendships have lasted more from the staying power of one friend than from the investment of both. That stalwart friend might be you. Maybe you put in more time, initiate the correspondence, make sure the meetups are planned, and are always there to support your friend.

---

[3] Chapman, G. The 5 Love Languages (First edition). Northfield Publishing, 2015

Why do some of us continue investing in relationships where we have the lion's share of the responsibilities? It might be that this total commitment is what we desire for ourselves. By exemplifying what we desire, we hope the other will take notice and reciprocate.

Another reason might be our belief that half a loaf is better than no bread. In other words, if we sever the friendship, we will be left with nobody, or at least nobody whom we want as much. So, we settle, not satisfied, but hang on because we are afraid to be left alone.

This brings us back to the importance of understanding each other's love language. Let's imagine that one of your close friends was asked to rate her degree of satisfaction with your friendship on a scale of 1-10 (with 10 being the most satisfactory). And let's say she rated your relationship a 6 or 7. How would you feel?

Let's complicate the above example a bit more. What if the friend, who, in your opinion, is a minimal contributor to maintaining the friendship, was the one who gave you this average rating?

Before you start venting all your years of pent-up angst, consider this: It is possible that despite all you do for your friend, she may not feel loved because you are doing for her what you would want to be done for yourself. You're not showing your love for her in a language she recognizes and appreciates.

The women who have maintained solid, equally invested friendships will tell you that these relationships take time and effort. We understand our friends' needs and do what we can, as often as we can, to meet those needs. Quality Time (75%), Acts of Service (58%), and Words of Affirmation (41%) were the top 3 preferred love languages of our respondents.

Next time you get together with your friends, bring a copy of Chapman's book and ask about their love languages. Share your own. If they look at you quizzically, you can say you're doing some research. This information can help enrich already great relationships and improve those that need an overhaul. If your friend is not prepared to invest in you, or if you are in a state of perpetual dissatisfaction, it's time to re-assess your reliance on that friend (And if this statement sounds repetitive, it is because it is meant to be. It's that important!).

Keeping in Touch

In addition to knowing how our friends wish to be appreciated and loved (love languages), our deep friendships, the ones we truly treasure, will not continue to thrive without a fair amount of personal investment. This includes spending time together, supporting, sharing, and keeping in touch. However, what is important to note is that each female friendship will differ in what this investment looks like.

Take communication, for example. Some friends do not engage in weekly or even monthly contact, but when they do get together, they feel like no time has passed, and they simply pick up where they left off. Others want daily or weekly communication to maintain their sense of connectedness.

47% of our respondents indicate that they communicate with their treasured friends weekly, 19% daily, and 13% monthly. Others, like this respondent, are pretty comfortable with less contact: *"As we have gotten older or found ourselves on different paths and responsibilities, we have less time for each other. As a result, we try to create quality time meetings at least once yearly."*

There are no hard and fast rules here. The easiest and simplest thing is to ask your friend if the current 'keeping in touch' level is satisfactory. If yes, keep it as is. If not, find out how frequently she would like to hear from you. She might want to hear from you more or less than you are willing to. Find a middle ground that you both can live with.

The Impact of Life Events

Moves, marriages, parenthood, deaths: all these significant events impact our lives personally and have repercussions on our friendships. These are the events at which we want our treasured friends beside us to celebrate or mourn—together.

Wouldn't it be great if all the significant events in our lives and that of our friends lined up evenly? We move simultaneously to the same place, get married around the same time, and have children at the same time in lockstep with each other. For some friends, this has happened, but not for most. One person could be going through a highly acrimonious divorce while her friend's committed relationship is flourishing. One friend could be experiencing difficulties getting pregnant while you pop out a child every two years. Can your friendship survive this?

So many life events can impact our friendships. But the truism that says you cannot prevent bad things from happening, but you can choose how you allow them to impact you, can also apply to our friendships. We cannot and should not be expected to solve all the problems affecting our friends' lives. However, we can stand in the gap beside them and support them as much as possible. Sometimes that is enough. Sometimes it's not.

Parenting

One respondent explained how being at different points in parenting, for example, affected her friendships:

> *"For me, a lot of resetting friendship priorities... culminated... in the last couple of years upon the birth of my second child. Two kids meant I needed to refocus more energy on my family. My ability to travel and see friends dramatically diminished. I felt let down that some of my friends didn't reciprocate when I needed them more. Parenting can sometimes be isolating and lonely because it is so crazy-making and full-on. Prioritizing friendships with folks who may have only one child or older children has been challenging."*

Parenting, with its all-encompassing demands, can mire the friend going through it that she has nothing left to give, even to immediate family members. A friend who understands this and is there to support her will be appreciated. Gifts, including food, presents, time—or anything to help the new or repeat mother cope during those early weeks, months, and years—are treasured.

But there are instances when parenting can negatively impact female friendships. Your friend may never emerge from her total involvement in her role as mother, leaving no time or space for you. She might even be affronted at your lack of understanding that her child needs to be first. What do you do?

One respondent recommends balance to ensure our friends are not cut off forever:

> *"Some friends, after they had kids, decided that less contact is better. This puts strain on relationships because it shows what is most important. I think there needs to be a balance between family time, friend time, and work time."*

Another recommends acceptance. Life is just like that:

> *"I wouldn't say that my life events have negatively affected my close friendships. They've just changed it. For example, my friend had a baby, and after that, I realized and accepted that there are going to be some events that she won't make it to or be able to stay out late, and for group trips, she won't be able to come unless she can bring the baby, too. I'm okay with that because I see babies as blessings, and she gave me my godson. I've navigated these transitions by acknowledging that it's a part of life, and I will continue to be there for my friends throughout these life events just like I know they will continue to be there for me."*

Again, we will respond differently because we are different people with different needs. However, if we want our friendships to continue to thrive, supporting our friends through life changes should be an important priority.

If time has passed and you're still consistently feeling neglected, talk to them about how you're feeling. There are no guarantees that the discussion will get you what you want, but at the very least, you will be able to hear each other's perspectives.

Moving Away

Relocation to a different town, city, province, or country might mean you have to plan further ahead for get-togethers, meet online, or direct message more frequently to keep the relationship strong. Yet, many female friendships do not survive when distance separates them. The loss is not always attributable to distance per se; it might have to do with the time of life one makes a move, the number of years the friendship spanned before the move, or the level of commitment from each friend involved.

New places expose us to new people to become invested in, sometimes leaving little or no room for those we left behind. Deep-seated friendships with solid roots and entrenched heart tentacles will be less impacted by distance. They compensate for what they lose in frequency or quantity of time spent together with a deeper level of conversations and sharing. Here's how one respondent coped with this issue:

> *"Getting married and relocating to different cities resulted in less frequent communication. Overall, the friendship is still strong because we communicate regularly and know we are still there for each other when we need it."*

Committed Relationships and Marriages

Significant-other relationships will always affect our friendships. This doesn't mean we can't have thriving friendships and a significant other. But it does mean that as we grow closer and build a future with our partner, it will inevitably affect the amount of time we share and the level of closeness we have with our friends.

You can disclose everything to your friends when you're dating. You can talk about intimate moments, bad dates, who paid for dinner, what you wore, what your date said, and how you felt.

But when building a trusting relationship with a long-term partner, you have to keep some things private. Building trust with a significant other means that they should be able to tell you things that don't get shared with others, including your best friend.

In a healthy, long-term relationship, you also spend time with each other's family and friends and share your social lives.

So, the time you once spent with your friends and family could easily get cut in half because now you have to divide your time between two different social circles. And there are only so many evenings and weekends in a year.

You and your significant other will also likely spend some of your vacation time together to create shared experiences and get to know each other in different settings. Most people don't have the luxury of having unlimited vacation time throughout the year, so it stands to reason that you will have less vacation time to go on trips with your girlfriends.

Lastly, in a healthy long-term relationship, you should plan for your future together—from which event you will attend on New Year's Eve to which city you plan to live. This will inevitably affect your friendships because they may no longer factor into your plans as much as they did when you were single.

You might wonder, "Does this mean that your friendships always have to change when you have a long-term partner?" They do, but that doesn't mean there aren't countless ways to maintain and strengthen your friendships as you navigate this change in your life.

How to Stay Invested in Your Friendships

We've shared the fundamentals about the changes your friendships will likely face over time, but there are many ways to keep your friends as an essential part of your life. Here are some ways to continue to invest in your friendships even as you build a solid and healthy partnership with your significant other.

When you're in a relationship, the first thing you can consider is that you don't have to strictly spend time with just you or your partner's social circle. There are lots of occasions where the two groups can mix. For example, when you plan to go to a music festival, there's usually no reason to keep the plans to just one person's group of friends. The more you mix your social circles, the more time you will have to spend with the important people in your life.

In a perfect world, you and your friends will have a significant other at the same time where you can go on double dates whenever you like, but that's not always (or even usually) the way life works. And some people choose to be single, so it's unrealistic to think you should only include your friends in your plans when they're also paired up. Try to think of ways to have your close friends in your plans regardless of whether they're single or paired up. When planning an event or outing for a group, it's also good to think about including more than one single friend so that no one feels like the odd one out in a group of couples.

One of the other ways friendships tend to change as you build your life with a significant other is that, as time goes on, you and your friends will have fewer shared experiences. You might default to just "catching each other up" on your lives instead of having experiences together. To invest in your friendships, you should consider ways to continue to experience your life with your friends instead of just telling them about it while they become bystanders.

One way to do this is to continue to plan some trips or vacations with your friends. Maybe you don't get to take two annual trips to Spain—one with your significant other and one with your friends—but can you plan a weekend together in a neighbouring city? Or perhaps plan a short road trip over a couple of days? When creating shared experiences and spending quality time together, you don't have to fly around the world or take two weeks off work to invest in your friendships. Making plans to see a concert or attend an event in your city can create a shared experience that is key to maintaining a solid friendship.

You can also create some rituals around what you and your friends love to do together. Perhaps you can do a spa day together every winter (A DIY spa day at one of your homes can be an excellent way to do this on a budget!). Putting a ritual in place can remind you to make time for your friends even as you default to making plans with your significant other.

A big part of creating closeness includes mutual self-disclosure. While it's true that you can't share those things that you or your partner prefer to keep private, it's still important to share your life with your friends. Talking to your friends about your plans, career, experiences, and feelings are all great ways to stay a part of each other's lives.

Even though many of your future plans probably won't be centred on your friendships, you can still share what your plans are (as long as they're not deemed private by your significant other). This is part of the continued mutual self-disclosure that ensures you and your friend can maintain closeness.

It's also up to you to advocate for the time you want to spend with your friends when having discussions with your significant other. If you're going to maintain strong friendships, then your significant other needs to be aware of your plans to nurture your friendships, and you can find ways to make room for them together.

Emilia

I've noticed an interesting pattern in some of my friendships where we began sharing our time with the friend's significant other. This isn't a bad thing in and of itself, mainly because it increases the amount of time my friends have available to spend with me, but I realized that it affected our level of self-disclosure. There are some things I prefer not to share with my friend's significant other. It helped me see that it's essential to carve out time with my friend one-on-one so that my friend and I can confide in each other.

Reflecting on your friendships, are there friends you need to plan some one-on-one time with? Experiment with different plans and see how that can sometimes change the dynamic.

Acknowledging and Making Space for Feelings

It is crucial that you and your friend maintain room for each other's needs and feelings. When you're in a significant long-term relationship, you need to nurture that partnership. Your friend will also have needs as they pertain to your friendship. It's essential that you both find ways to ensure that you each feel supported, valued, and cared for. Regardless of the changes, your friendship will face, it's vital that you both hold compassion for each other's points of view.

Speaking up about your needs and feelings becomes harder the longer you leave them unaddressed and more complex when too much time passes without any sharing. Your needs will eventually become resentments if they go unvoiced and unmet. For example, if you wait a year to tell your friend that you've been feeling neglected, they'll feel blind-sided, and your friendship's trust will be negatively affected. Resentments tend to build up over time, causing the friendship to become harder to repair.

Sometimes what gets in the way of sharing our feelings can be that our friend is having an opposite emotional experience. They might be swimming in bliss while you're drowning in sadness. You might feel like you don't want to dampen your friend's joy, or your joyful friend might not think it's fair to put their bliss aside to talk you through your hard feelings. So how do you navigate that?

First and foremost, make sure that you're sitting with, acknowledging, and making space for your feelings. Sometimes, without realizing it, we want our friends to validate how we're feeling, but we don't do it for ourselves. If we don't learn to sit with our feelings and comfort ourselves, our emotional states will always clash with our friends, meaning that there won't be room for both sets of feelings when they differ. When that happens, we will either have to override or neglect our feelings or impose our negative emotional state on our friends.

Emilia

Here is an example of how I met and soothed my tough feelings in my own life. My friend and I had plans to get together for lunch shortly after she became engaged. Her engagement brought up lots of feelings for me. It brought up my fears about finding someone to share my life with as well as feelings of shame and unworthiness around being single. However, in that important meeting when my friend and I got together after one of the best moments of her life, I wanted to create a safe space for my friend's happiness to land.

So, before we met up, I took a moment of stillness and allowed what I felt. I acknowledged my feelings of fear and unworthiness. I held my hand to my heart and said to myself, "It's ok that I feel this way. I'm allowed to feel scared and have feelings of doubt. My feelings are real, but that doesn't mean my fears will come true or that I am unworthy of finding a partner."

And then, I set the intention to be present for my friend, share in her excitement, and support her in that moment. Supporting her meant that I chose not to voice my fears on this occasion or somehow lessen her excitement with my response to her. On this day, at this moment, I would create a safe space for my friend's happiness to land with me. But what was key about this is that I didn't push away the difficult feelings I was experiencing in myself.

In contrast, seven years prior, when my friend Scarlett got engaged, I had convinced myself that I wasn't afraid or feeling unworthy in order to avoid facing these tough feelings. I overrode my feelings with thoughts that I didn't quite buy into about how my single life was amazing. I would tell myself that I was having so much fun and that my friend's engagement did not affect my happiness or self-confidence. To override my feelings, I had to do everything to prove that I was happy. This meant going out with my single friends and spending as much time as I could with them. But when I spent time with my engaged friend, it moved my fears closer to the surface. And because I didn't acknowledge or validate my feelings, I couldn't be fully present and authentic with my friend.

To show my happiness for her, I ignored my fears and found ways to quiet them. As I pushed my feelings down, I wasn't being completely genuine with myself or my friend. And regardless of how hard I tried to act as though I was happy for her, she could tell that something was off. I was doing everything I was supposed to, but the underlying feelings of heartfelt happiness weren't there. Over time, this created resentment for her and undermined our friendship.

From this, we conclude that you first have to honour your feelings before you can honour the feelings of others. To create a safe space for your friend's feelings, you need to create a safe space to hold yours. And you can only do this by being honest and compassionate with yourself. Creating a safe space also means that when you communicate hurt feelings, you ensure that your communication is not volatile or reactive. This is possible when you've met and managed your feelings first.

Transitioning into a committed relationship or marriage seems to hit female friendships the hardest of all life events. One respondent described how her friend became too busy to connect with her after getting married. On the other hand, she found a balance when she got married. But even though she tried to connect, her friend always made an excuse. Eventually, she stopped trying:

Connection is a two-way street. I'd be happy to connect if she wants to and makes an effort to reach out.

Something about losing your BFF to another who takes the priority—the leaving and cleaving ministers invoke upon newlyweds that are assumed once a relationship becomes intensely exclusive—can trigger reactions from the friend left behind. For some, it happens in the early days:

My friendship ended with one friend because of her wedding. She was shockingly self-centred.

For others, it's more like a gradual shift:

I found a shift in some of my female friendships when I entered a committed relationship. I could have handled this transition more gracefully. Still, it also coincided partially with the death of someone close in my life, and it was a perfect storm of changing circumstances, where I clung to the support of my partner versus my female friends.

Also, when our female friends link up with those we do not think are good for them, it is hard to smile and pretend. This is genuinely a no-win scenario. You might be accused of being unsupportive or even jealous if you criticize the chosen partner. If you don't say anything negative, you might be accused of not warning your friend if things take a bad turn. Some friends might even cut ties with each other until things change. In the example below, once the marriage dissolved, the friendship resumed:

My friends did not like my husband (He didn't like them much either but certainly pretended to as we were getting together). As the marriage continued, it affected my friendships, and I didn't see many of them. Since the divorce, my relationships with my close friends have improved greatly.

And yet, in other cases, navigating the transition to a committed relationship and balancing that with time for friends proved too challenging:

When I married, I could not meet all my best friends because I was too busy with my family. I could not navigate the transition well, so I became unhappy. I divorced 9.5 years later. Even after my divorce, I could not navigate the transition well because I had to focus on myself and manage my transition for myself.

Learning to navigate transitions is what life events force onto all of us. And it seems that some people are better equipped to handle the change than others.

In reviewing the responses from our survey group, there is an implication in the data that the life events we would consider favourable (parenting, marriages, and even relocation to a new place with new opportunities) had more negative impacts on friendships than adverse events (divorce and death). It's almost as if happiness in our female friends' lives highlights the things lacking in our own. But when there is a loss, we rally around each other, joined and unified against a fate that no amount of whistling in the dark can prevent.

Trauma makes you realize who your real friends are.

It doesn't have to be so. We can choose to be the kind of friends who are there for each other through the good and bad times.

Maintenance for the Long Haul or the Shorter Run

While the focus of this book is primarily on the friendships that have stood the test of time throughout the years, we mustn't ignore the 'shorter run' types. If we think back to our past and the people to whom we attached the label 'friends,' we usually discover a few who were only in our lives for a short period of time. Perhaps they were with us in high school, during university, or at a particular juncture in our lives. And during that period, they loomed largely. However, as life took us to new places and new people, these people faded out of our lives as we grew and changed.

The information described in earlier chapters regarding what draws people together also comes into play here. We do not usually know at the outset if a friendship will be short- or long-term. We might be drawn together due to a shared problem or pressing situation. Perhaps you meet a woman in your gym or Lamaze class, and voilà, you hit it off. For the duration of that situation or period, you two are inseparable. Until you're not.

One respondent captured the sentiment well:

> "*My friend once said there are three kinds of friends, and all three are important: friends for a reason, friends for a season, and friends forever. All friendships matter, and just because someone is not a forever friend doesn't mean the friendship wasn't valuable.*"

- **Friends for a reason:** These women are placed in our lives to teach us things and help us grow in ways we could not have grown without their influence. For the sake of illustration, let's look at an example:

Jennifer will tell you that Brooke saved her sanity. As a new manager in a highly competitive company, Jennifer could not get her colleagues to take her ideas seriously, even though she was a hard worker. She got talked over, ignored, and sidelined. However, soft-spoken Brooke listened when Jennifer talked. She could calmly quiet a room and create opportunities for Jen to share her ideas. She openly championed the good ones, ensuring Jennifer got credit as well.

Before that, Jennifer had never met a strong, quiet leader. She would go home, especially after a workday full of meetings, and beat herself up for letting the other sales managers, most of them men, steamroll her and treat her like an assistant. Brooke befriended her, and for the three years they worked together, she showed her how to fight for her voice to be heard. When Brooke moved onto a different job, Jennifer missed her and never forgot how she helped her grow in ways she would not have dreamed.

- **Friends for a season:** These friendships work well during a time of need or a particular life passage. An example could look like this:

Helene met Genevieve at a divorce recovery therapy session. Both were reeling from the transition and trying to manage as primary parents of young children. Helene's story so mirrored Genevieve's that they got together after that first class to commiserate over coffee. By the end of the evening, they had exchanged phone numbers. They supported each other through play dates, park picnics, crying fits, meetings with lawyers, and more crying fits. When Genevieve secured a much-needed, higher-paying job, she had little time left to spend with Helene. Finding a new place so that she could live closer to her work did not help matters either. Promises were made to keep in touch, but life's busyness made those promises impossible to keep. Genevieve refused to let things fade with Helene without an acknowledgement. She wrote a touching letter to Helene expressing her gratitude for the friendship that supported her during a difficult period. Helene received it and was touched. She felt the same way. They were both in different places in their lives and couldn't stay close to each other, but their friendship was no less meaningful.

- **Friends forever:** These are proven, tried, and tested friendships. There's history here, strong binding ties that very little in life can shake. These are the 'ride or die' women friends. Here's an illustrative example:

Anessa, with her skinny chest heaving and nose bleeding, did more damage to the bully who had purposefully knocked Suubi's lunch to the cafeteria floor. Defiant even as they were being hauled into the principal's office, she still attempted to rain fists on the boy dangling from the other arm of the arresting teacher, daring him to another fight so she could teach him a lesson about picking on people half his size. Suubi fell in love right then and there with this feisty, skinny, barely 5-foot-tall girl who only grew an additional 3 inches into adulthood. When Anessa lost her mother to Ebola, Suubi stood by her. When Suubi graduated from medical school, Anessa, decorated with tattoos and riding a motorcycle, rode Suubi around the city at high speed to celebrate. They were sisters, bonded from that day in the cafeteria. Each knew the other was just a call away—friends for life.

For a reason, season, or for life, we can benefit and grow from each type of friendship; we could not leave this chapter on friendship maintenance without acknowledging them. Each type requires an investment of our time. Each type should be celebrated, even the ones that ended badly. Once we look past the hurt, we will see how that person forced us to grow, laugh, and share a place in time with them so we would not feel alone on the planet.

Maybe it's time to write a letter of thanks as Genevieve did. If you have never done so, let these 'season' and 'reason' women know how much you value their contributions to your life.

Key Learning

- Friendships require an investment of time.
- Learning the love languages of our friends can enrich our relationships and ensure they feel appreciated and loved.
- Life events will impact your friendships.
- Not all friends are meant to be in your life forever, but that's okay. We can find much to celebrate even in those friendships that are just for a season.

Discussion Questions

1. Do we always know which friends are for life and which will be short-term?
2. What rating of closeness would you give your current friendships?
3. What role do you play in maintaining your friendships?
4. Do you think you need your friends more than they need you (or vice versa)?
5. Which past friend would you most likely reach out to with a letter of thanks?
6. Is there a yearning for a specific type of friendship you cannot seem to land?
7. Have you and a close friend ever experienced a time when one of you was happy, and the other was unhappy? How did this play out in your friendship? Is there anything you think you should have done differently to make space for both of your feelings?

8. If you're in a committed relationship right now, what ways can you continue to strengthen your friendships? (Choose one thing and commit to doing that in the next month).
9. If your closest friend is in a committed relationship, are you happy with how your friendship is going? Do you think there are any needs you should voice?

Is It Time to Break Up?

"Take note of how people treat you; invest your time in those who uplift you."

It's a fact of life that the closer we get to someone, the more vulnerable we are to potentially getting hurt. You can't get close to someone without trusting them and letting your guard down. But your self-preservation instincts might sometimes kick in when a friend lets you down or disappoints you. To avoid getting hurt again, you might ask yourself: should I forgive this person or just move on from this friendship altogether?

Maybe you're considering this question because someone has hurt you, or perhaps you feel the relationship is one-sided and you're the one putting in all the effort. Regardless of the reason, how can you decide whether to forgive someone, work on the relationship, or end the friendship?

Evaluating the Friendship

When determining the answer to this question, you should first ask yourself whether you can trust this person.

Trusting means you are willing to believe that this person didn't intentionally hurt or neglect you. Continuing a friendship where you don't trust the other person isn't fair to the other person, and you won't get much fulfillment from it either. But if you can trust each other, you can discuss the issues you've experienced and how you can work together to solve them.

The next question to consider is if you have voiced your disappointment or stated your needs yet.

Sometimes we convince ourselves that our friend should know how we are feeling. But you must be honest with yourself—is it fair to expect this? Or is it an excuse you're using so that you don't have to deal with a potentially uncomfortable conversation?

If your friend has demonstrated her care for you in the past, you should give her the benefit of the doubt and try to voice your needs, hurt, or disappointment in a kind, clear, and direct way. It's best to use a recent example if you've experienced a recurring problem and try not to generalize too much. Once you've communicated your hurt feelings, you can assess how open your friend is to listening to your grievances and repairing the relationship.

If you've been honest and patient with your friend, and you're still not completely happy with the friendship, you should definitely do some more reflection. Here are some crucial questions to ask yourself when you're determining whether the friendship is worth your continued effort and care:

1. How do you feel when you're in her company? Do you mostly feel good around her?
2. Do you trust her? Why or why not?
3. Do you feel appreciated by her? Why or why not?
4. Do you feel respected?
5. Do you feel valued?

6. Do you feel understood?
7. Do you feel she is receptive to what you need?
8. Do you feel as though your friendship is usually equal in effort?
9. Does this friendship have a positive effect on your well-being?

If you answered yes to the above questions, the friendship is worth your effort, time, and love.

That said, not everyone has the exact needs and values regarding friendships, so here are some additional questions you can reflect on. It's up to you to decide if these things are important to you:

1. Can you have deep discussions with her?
2. Are there activities that you can both enjoy together?
3. Do you have any similar interests?
4. Do you have a history that you would like to honour and continue?

These questions will help you reflect on what's important to you and what you think are good reasons to invest in the friendship. You will then be equipped to decide what to do next.

Very often, as per the responses in our survey, women don't verbalize friendship breakups. They just decrease contact with the person. This might be because of a fear of confrontation, but it's also possible that not every breakup needs to be verbalized—especially when you've voiced your grievances, which were never resolved. You might choose to honour the friendship for what it was but create different boundaries to protect your happiness and time. This will also give you more time to invest in other relationships that positively contribute to your life.

Another thing to consider when it comes to potential friendship breakups is that life's only constant is change. Take note however, that not all friendships are equipped to deal with change.

If you have been friends with someone for a long time, you may have met your friend when you were young. We tend to become friends with people who share our interests, but when we are young, these interests tend to be determined by our circumstances. We live where our families want us to live, go to school where our families want us to go to school, and do what our families want us to do. And we become friends with the people who find themselves where we live and where we go to school.

As we get older, we have many more options available to us. We have more information, a greater awareness of our preferences, and more autonomy to act on those preferences. Our priorities become entirely our own. Our lives will inevitably change when we have new options and autonomy. And as we pursue our life path, it is very likely that we, ourselves, will change.

And as our lives change, our friendships will inevitably change. It is usually in these times of change that you will be able to see the foundation of your friendship. Was your friendship circumstantial, or was it based in conscious effort?

Circumstantial vs. Conscious Effort Friendships

When you come up against changes in your friendships—the ways you relate, the things you have in common, how you spend time together, and how much time you spend together—you will inevitably face conflict. There will be times when the way you think won't align with the way your friend thinks.

If your friendship is based in conscious effort, it will likely consist of honesty, openness, collaboration regarding each other's needs, and a willingness to invest effort. It will probably stand the test of time. If your friendship is only circumstantial, you will find that it might not have the glue to sustain the changes you will face in your life.

Even if a friendship is more circumstantial, you can take steps to continue the friendship with conscious effort. But first, you need to figure out whether you would like to actively pursue the friendship and if your friend is willing to actively pursue the friendship with you. Consciously pursuing the friendship will usually mean increasing your friendship's honesty, collaboration, and effort.

Forgiving Your Friends

Now that you've reflected on your friendship(s), let's discuss what it can look like if you decide to pursue it and do the work of forgiving your friend for any disappointment or hurt you experienced that may have brought you to this fork in the road.

Sometimes when a friend does something that hurts you, your mind won't let you forget it. Your mind will release angering memories and negative thoughts to keep you safe. Your mind will colour the person's every action and word with a negative assumption to protect you from further hurt. It can take a lot of effort to let go and forgive because your subconscious mind can sometimes rebel against your intention.

Sometimes this can be resolved when you regain your own trust. You read that right—sometimes, it's not your friend that needs to regain your trust; it's you that needs to regain your own trust.

Your mind is rebelling against forgiveness because it doesn't trust *you* to keep *you* safe.

The first step in regaining your own trust is to take responsibility. When you reflect on your conflict with your friend, what is your part in the situation? Where can you take ownership of what happened? When you reflect on this, you can feel more empowered to protect yourself from future hurt.

Usually, when there is a recurring issue in a relationship, we somehow contribute to the problem. To this, you might say: that's not true. If my friend does something repeatedly that upsets me, I don't believe it's my fault.

Certainly, it's not your fault, but how could you have contributed to the problem? Did you communicate your needs specifically while staying open to what they were experiencing and needing?

Make sure you always consider how your actions, or even a lack of boundaries, might contribute to a recurring issue.

So, what was your part in the situation?

Emilia

When I was 30 years old, I endured a terrible breakup and lost my job just two months later. In the months following, I lost a good friend to cancer, and my grandfather passed away. My closest friend at the time had moved in with her boyfriend and was at the happiest point in her life. It was a devastating time for me, and I felt completely abandoned by her in a time of great need because she prioritized her relationship and left little thought and time for me. After some time and introspection (and a few trips to the therapist's office), I had an epiphany.

I had tried to build security outside of myself by over-giving to my friendship. Subconsciously, I had attended to my friend so fervently when she was going through hard times because I wanted to secure the same kind of care for myself when I needed it. That doesn't mean that I am not a good friend who didn't empathize with what my friend was going through or that I was helping her with a purely selfish heart. But I had to admit and take ownership of the fact that I was so devastated when it seemed like my friend abandoned me in my time of need because I had been there for her when she was going through difficult times.

I didn't realize that I set myself up for failure and disappointment when I gave to guarantee support when I needed it. When I tried to bank the care and self-sacrifice I offered, it led to later disappointment and resentment. Ironically, disappointment and resentment make it difficult to receive support and care, even when provided.

Another question to ask yourself: is there something you are feeling underneath this hurt and anger? For example, envy. If your friend has something you wish for in your life, perhaps your negative reactions repress the truth. Maybe the truth is that your friend has something that you're afraid of not being able to achieve for yourself.

This is something that happened to me. When my friend's relationship became serious, and she and her boyfriend moved in together and started shopping for houses, I rejected her presence in my life and coloured her actions with negative assumptions. Deep down, I was afraid that I couldn't have those things—a loving relationship and a successful life that included a house of my own.

By having hostile reactions to your friend, you are actually pushing away the very thing you want. You are reinforcing your low self-worth in a certain area. Instead of seeking ways to get closer to what you want and affirming that you can have it, you will resist the very reality you desire.

This is all to say that it's in your best interest to parse through your feelings. Feeling envious can lead to shame, a powerful emotion that feels like the truth. Most people will push shame away at all costs, and one of the easiest ways is to fool yourself into thinking that you don't even want what you envy. And in your mind, you will judge and reject the person who has what you envy.

Releasing Negative Emotions

There is no easy route to forgiveness, but the most important thing is to reflect on how your actions and feelings might have contributed to the issue. After all, you might choose to end a friendship or keep it, but you will always be the common denominator in any friendship you have. For this reason, it is crucial to reflect on what you can do to ensure that the friendships in your life are mutually gratifying, supportive, and caring.

If you've spent time reflecting and have decided to end your friendship, you can choose to tell the person why you are ending your friendship or not. But if you do decide to verbalize your breakup, keep in mind that unleashing your anger on someone thoughtlessly isn't productive or kind. And perhaps it's better to remember your values and honour your friendship with a parting that doesn't injure the other person emotionally.

Whether or not you choose to verbalize your breakup, writing a letter is an excellent method to process any anger you're experiencing. This can help you release your feelings, process what you've experienced, and give voice to your hurt and disappointment.

The audience of this letter can be your friend that hurt you, or it can just be a letter to yourself. Either way, hold back nothing. Be as candid and direct as possible. Share how you are feeling. Document how long you have felt this way and identify how your friend's behaviour made you feel. Write until there is nothing left to say.

Here is a working guide. I've provided some examples, but you can personalize them for your situation:

1. **Acknowledge why you are writing this letter:**

   Dear (name),

   You may never read these words I am about to write, but now that I have had a little time to get some perspective, I want to fully express how I feel about what has transpired between us.

2. **Describe what the person did and how it made you feel:**

   I am really pissed off at you right now. More than that, however, I am hurt, disappointed, frustrated, and upset with myself. I'm mad at myself for giving you so much power to hurt me. Angry for putting up with your selfishness over the years, hoping for change, and being naive enough to believe your promises to do better...

3. **Describe your next step:**

   I have finally gotten some sense. Enough already. I need and deserve people in my life who will uplift me, support me, and love me, not only for what I can give them but for who I am. I want a friend who will put my needs above her own—not for what she can get in return, but because she sincerely wants what's best for me. And not what is always convenient for her. That's what true friends do. You were never that friend. So, I am letting you go. One day I might look back on this experience and be thankful, but right now, it's time for me to get on with my life without you. Goodbye.

You can then read the letter to an empty chair. Afterward, you can either burn it or keep it as a reminder so you're not tempted to return to that friendship.

Breaking up with a friend is hard. But sometimes, it is what you must do to preserve your peace of mind and happiness, especially after trying other options.

Key Learning

- When deciding whether to end a friendship, the first step is to consider whether you can trust the other person.
- Further reflection can include how the person makes you feel and whether they positively contribute to your well-being.
- Forgiving a friend can be difficult if we don't repair our trust in ourselves.
- We need to take ownership of how we contribute to recurring issues in our friendships.
- A gradual reduction in contact is how most women prefer to break up with friends.

Discussion Questions

1. Is there a friend that you are considering breaking up with?
2. When you consider the list of questions in this chapter, what do you think contributes most to your feelings?
3. Beneath the reasons why you're considering a breakup, what are the feelings you are experiencing?
4. After reading this chapter, are you more certain of the breakup, or do you think your friendship can be repaired?

Friendship Advice

"A truly dependable friend is everything; to me, that friend is you."

The women, averaging more than 25 years of friendships, who gave us such inspirational fodder for this book also provided helpful advice for younger women about female friendships. Below, their responses have been summarized into categories. To preserve authenticity, we have kept each piece of advice as closely as possible to the original words written by the respondent.

Words of Advice

1. **Be the friend you want to have.**

- Be a good friend: a giver, not just a receiver; balance what they need with your needs.
- Be open-minded and forgiving.
- Build trust, and be kind, honest, and respectful.
- Be patient; be willing to take a back seat at times; be supportive; enjoy the benefits.
- Take time to understand yourself and set your standards and boundaries. Know when you would be willing to

compromise and be flexible, and do not treat all your friends the same way. Treat them as individuals.

- Be open-minded and fair.
- Always be yourself and do not change yourself to fit in with anyone.
- Self-love is the key to being a good friend. Know yourself and who you are (don't worry, you don't have to figure it all out right away—and you won't—it's an ongoing journey) and be secure with that. The best way to make good friends is to give them a little of yourself (show some vulnerability), and they will hopefully give some back. You will have trust and a foundation to build your friendships on from there.
- REMEMBER, whatever you look for in a friend, YOU SHOULD FIRST BE. "You should first show yourself friendly."
- You can only be a good friend if you are also a good friend to yourself. Always listen, keep an open mind, and don't judge.
- Be a friend firstly to yourself. Do not expect perfection; your friend is human like you, and she will sometimes disappoint you, and you may become disillusioned. Like any relationship, you have to work at it and remember the need for boundaries as you seek to develop your female relationships.

2. **Be careful in your selection.**

   - Pick your circle carefully.
   - Don't make friends indiscriminately.
   - Choose friends who share the same values as you.
   - Don't be somebody else to be accepted; real friends are okay with who you are—good, bad, vulnerable, quirky, etc.

- Follow your gut. If you feel a connection, if that person is a good listener, lifts you when you're down, and isn't all about herself—you have a good friend.
- Don't be afraid to let go of what doesn't serve you. You don't owe it to anyone. When you're supported, seen, and heard, magic can happen. You deserve that, and you deserve to share that space with others.
- Give yourself time to know the person to discover what they're about.
- Choose your female friends wisely with God's guidance. There are certain qualities to look for when choosing your female friends. They should be honest, understanding, loyal, trustworthy, etc. Female friendships are vital when you find them.
- Listen to yourself and your body's responses around friends.
- Choose your friends wisely because not every acquaintance is a friend. Choose people who respect you and lift you up, whom you can do the same for.
- Be selective with whom you call a friend. You need female friends who are trustworthy, loyal, honest, and understanding because they'll be the ones that you talk to about anything. You also need female friends who help protect your energy while you help protect theirs. You need to mirror everything you want your friends to be for you and be the same for them because there needs to be a balance for the friendship to thrive.

3. **Choose friends who will build you up.**

- *Never bring people in your life that do not bring joy, laughter, and* well-being; surround yourself with positive people.

- Let a friendship go if it's unhealthy and draining.
- You do not need a lot of female friends—just one who truly has your back.
- Don't allow anyone to stop you from being you.
- The people you want to be friends with are the ones that will not cause drama in your life.
- Find someone you get along with. Someone welcoming, kind, loving, empathetic, and shares most of your interests and values. Someone pleasant, respectful, and accepting of who you are. We are not perfect, but someone should at least possess some qualities we can tolerate.
- Have friends that support your ambitions and your well-being.
- True female friendship will prop you up, not tear you down.
- If you are consistently disappointed with a friend, you have to let them go. Some things can't be changed.

4. **Be prepared for changes and conflicts.**

- Friendships change at the stages of life you are in.
- Remember, some friendships are for a time, and some last longer.
- People come into your life during different seasons. Some will end up staying longer than others.
- Keep in touch. Life changes and reconnections are possible. Remain judgement-free.
- Don't run when things get complicated. People aren't easy to deal with. Neither are we. Love despite the flaws.
- Trust when broken takes effort to heal, but sometimes it never does. Forgiveness helps.

- Resolve conflicts. Don't ignore them. Lift each other up. Life is hard enough.
- Be there for a friend when life changes. It doesn't mean you have to be there physically.
- Focusing on minor arguments too much will impact the friendship, and that's not worth it. Accept that people make mistakes and might not always agree with you. This is good because the more diverse your friends are, the more you learn from them.
- Remember, no one is perfect.
- Choose wisely—these people could be in your life for a long time and affect your life decisions.

5. **Time investment is required.**

- Invest time in the relationship. Great female friendships come with hard work.
- It takes work to maintain healthy and strong bonds.
- Value your friendships and put in the effort sometimes. It's not always easy.
- The best friendships take a lot of time to develop into lasting relationships!
- Check in with your close friends: see if they're doing okay, and don't assume how they feel.
- Invest in one-on-one time, and don't let your love life get in the way!
- You will meet many people in your life. But when you feel a connection with someone, you need to hold it tight and water it so it can grow. Send a text. Do something nice. Show that you care.

- Even if life takes you far, keep in touch, and make sure you grow together.
- Consider investing your time and energy in people who will do the same.
- Keep in touch, at least monthly.
- Keep your female friends close and make the time, even if you think you lack it. Life is long and unexpected, and you can't begin to anticipate the curveballs it will throw your way. The stronger your safety net of amazing and trusted female friends is, the softer your landing will be. Be kind and understanding of your friends' changing circumstances and welcome them back into the fold—even if they moved to a different city for the boy they fell in love with. Go to Vegas together at least once in your life to reminisce about dancing on rooftops when you're both old and grey, smelling faintly of mothballs, and lives well lived.

6. **Communicate.**

- Ask for help.
- Communication is key. Dive deep into topics that aren't just about parties and makeup so you can better understand each other. Female friendships are meaningful because they can help you grow as a woman in ways that intimate relationships can't.
- Say what's on your mind, ALWAYS! Don't be afraid to tell your friends how you feel.
- Be very transparent in everything you do, and if there are disagreements, address and do not ignore them. This will avoid conflicts.
- Don't be afraid to be open and friendly with new people.
- Foster them, cherish them, and hold them close.

- Offer an ear and send a little gift—make sure she knows she can turn to you if needed.
- Open communication will keep your friendship growing. Resolve conflicts. Don't ignore them.
- Be willing to accept; constructive criticism isn't always necessary.

7. **Accept your friends for who they are.**

- Know your friends and accept them with their faults and all.
- Teach each other and learn FROM each other.
- Don't sweat the small stuff. Assume good intent and exhibit good intent, as this is the only way to establish trust.
- Some will disappoint you, but many will love you.
- Let them know who you are. Let them decide if that suits them.
- Don't try to compete with her; just try to root for her. Be straightforward without being mean or rude.
- Do not expect perfection: your friend is human like you, and she will sometimes disappoint you, and you may become disillusioned.
- Love yourself enough to have friends that accept you as you, who feed you with positivity and push you to make wise decisions.
- Be yourself, be honest. If it's a real friendship, it will make you be and feel better. If not, it's not a friendship; it's a power struggle.

8. **Shared gender can be empowering.**

- Hold your female friendships close. They will be very dear to you, and you will find that female support is a powerful source of energy that lifts you.

- Nobody can understand you better than another woman.

- It's so important to have close female friends because they provide an outlet for you to grow personally and professionally. If they are really close, they become friends for life. They go through the various life stages with you, through your happy and sad times, and are always there for you.

- No matter how your life changes, always maintain good female friendships. You won't regret it.

- It is good to have other female perspectives on various life issues. It is essential to enhance our character as strong and confident wives, mothers, professionals, and mentors.

- [Female friendships] are critical. Our female friends teach us, support us, and add so much joy to our lives!

- Close female friends are always there for you: they share in your successes, joys, disappointments, and heartaches and give themselves always.

- Having female friendships will help you to become a better woman.

- I used to have more male friends, but I never felt allowed to be myself until I started really investing in my female friendships.

- [Female friendships] are complex and require as much honesty and presence as possible. I receive just as much, as well as a mirror, to understand the power of femininity.

- Having a female friend is like having a sister. You can share and be vulnerable with each other. You can party together and make memories. You laugh and enjoy each other. You cry together. It's one of the most special gifts you get.

9. **But all is not positive:** Females can be complicated. We would be doing an injustice to all the women who took the time to communicate their perspectives about female friendships if we did not share the negative comments. Not all women experience positive relationships with other women. Some have been burned, hurt, or just don't like other females as friends. For the record, here are some frank words of wisdom:

- Females tend to be quite fake. Honesty is hard to come by. So much emotion is involved in many things that you do. Very catty. Attempt to decide who should be your friend.
- Three women cannot be best friends.
- Women are more complicated than men.
- [Female friendships] don't usually last that long.
- Women are weird, and having many friends is overrated. Having a small set of friends or even just one close friend you can rely on is best.
- You cannot expect any friend to address all your needs and interests.
- Females who [are needy] are drawn close to me. I found it very difficult to maintain those relationships because many of those female friends were not interested in serving others but expected to be served.
- [Female friendships] are very needy and selfish.
- [Female friendships] are so complicated, and you can't hope to invest in every single one, so pick carefully.

- Women are very complex. Don't open your heart to everyone that appears they have your genuine interest at heart. Test the spirit.

What Does This Teach Us?

Communication, acceptance, selectivity, complexity, change, conflict, investment, reciprocity, support, empowerment, and gender solidarity are expected in our female friendships.

If we are honest with ourselves, we have all 'dropped the ball' at times with our friends. We may not have invested when we should have, chose not to be available at times, and within the busyness of life and the many balls we are juggling, it's a wonder some of our friendships have survived.

But there is that woman we call a friend who still calls us when we don't, keeps up their side and ours until we land at a better place in life, and crawls into bed beside and cries with us through our troubles. When we are weak, they stalwartly support us, and we are so very grateful for their presence.

Friendship contributions are not always 50/50. We know that. Sometimes you are always doing the propping-up and want someone to prop you up for a change. A good friend remains aware. She sees your giving, looks beyond your strength and affirms what she knows to be true of your presence in her life—that her wings would have less wind without you.

Key Learning

- Friends require a time investment.
- Communication is key to any relationship.
- Accept friends for who they are.
- Female friendships can be complicated.

Discussion Questions

1. Which of the above advice do you connect with the most?
2. Which area do you think you need to improve on within your existing friendships?
3. Based on your experience, would you add more words of wisdom to the above?
4. Do you agree that female friendships are complicated?
5. Write down five things you appreciate most about one of your treasured friends. What are you going to do with it?

Making New Friends

"Don't be afraid to be open and friendly with new people."

Many people find it more challenging to make friends once they're out of school and working full-time. No longer can we rely on being in the same classes and having similar schedules. Our careers may take us to a new city, or our friends' careers and relationships might whisk them away to different places. People's lives are at various stages, and the busyness of these life stages frequently leaves less room for friendships.

Making New Friends is a Process

If we find ourselves craving more female friendships in our lives, how can we begin the process of getting to know and befriending someone new?

Our survey indicated that 20% of respondents find it somewhat challenging to make new friends, and 10% find it difficult. Our survey results also demonstrated that 53% of respondents are interested in making new friends, and 39% are open to making new friends but are not necessarily actively looking.

It's also possible that those women who aren't actively trying to make new friends aren't trying because they're unsure where to start and are uncertain whether their efforts will be rewarded.

Emilia

Since the beginning of my career, I moved to cities where I didn't know many people. I had to build my social network from the ground up, and I did so consciously with determination.

Erin was one of the first people I met when I moved to Ottawa. She and I both attended a professional development session. I noticed she was about my age when she asked a question during the session. I approached her after the session, and we chatted. I told her I'd like to stay in touch, and we exchanged contact information. I messaged her the following day, and we planned to go for sushi.

This seems like a reasonably straightforward way to meet someone, but here are some of the usual stumbling blocks:

1. We say we want to make new friends but overlook the opportunities to do this. I kept my goal in mind, and when I saw someone about my age, I approached her and made conversation.
2. We tend to talk ourselves out of approaching someone because we wonder if the person will think we are strange, reject us, believe we are hitting on them, or any other possibility we fear.
3. We don't reach out after we have approached someone and exchanged contact information. You might have

thought, "I'll wait for this person to reach out to me—they have my information, too." But if everyone chooses to think this way, no one will make the first move, and new friendships won't form. So, don't be afraid to reach out first.

It's important to stay mindful of these potential stumbling blocks. What is really the worst-case scenario if you approach a potential new friend?

Emilia

I have approached many potential friends throughout my adulthood; in many cases, these people turned into long-time friends. Erin? She is still a close friend, and we are a stable source of support and encouragement for each other. I even visited her when she and her husband were posted to another country.

Of course, connections don't always turn into friends. But so what? I am so grateful for the times I took a chance because it led to wonderful friendships.

So why is it that sometimes we don't follow up once we exchange contact information with a potential new friend? Commonly we talk ourselves out of making the first move. I can tell you from experience that a subconscious fear of rejection drives that kind of inaction. We don't want to follow up because we fear the other person will not reciprocate our enthusiasm to get to know each other. But when you do it once or twice, you learn that most people are receptive, and when they don't, it's not actually that big of a deal, and we can choose not to take it personally.

I once tried to connect with someone, but she thought I was hitting on her. Does that say anything negative about me? No, it doesn't.

It is only telling of her personal biases and perspectives. Perhaps she wasn't open to meeting new people or new experiences. Or maybe she didn't trust that someone would want to be friends with her unless they had romantic motives. Or perhaps she just wasn't used to people reaching out and trying to make friends with her, so she didn't know what to think! Regardless, the interaction highlighted that I am an open person interested in making friends.

That scenario was the only somewhat negative experience I've had trying to make a friend. It wasn't a big deal, and now it's kind of a funny story to look back on!

Other times, connections just didn't stick. So, think about it. What do you have to lose in trying to make a new friend?

How to Make New Friends

Here is a list of unexpected ways I have made new friends. I hope this list shows you how many opportunities exist to meet people.

1. **Interviewing Roommates:**

   I interviewed roommates for my two-bedroom condo and met a woman I got along with very well. We seemed to have a lot in common. We didn't become roommates, but I told her I'd be interested in staying in touch. She later invited me to a Halloween party. When I attended her party, I met a woman who is still one of my closest friends. I took simple steps: I chatted with her at the party and let her know I'd like to stay in touch, then followed up and made plans. The friend who introduced us became more of an acquaintance because our schedules were very different, so we had difficulty staying in touch. But I made a new friend through her network!

My advice: *Follow up quickly with an invitation to get together so that the inspiration you feel to connect with your new acquaintance doesn't lose momentum. Friends of friends are great sources for new connections.*

2. **Attending a professional development conference:**

   Yvonne (the book's co-author!) and I met at a Career Development Practitioner Conference. She led a fantastic session on Getting Unstuck and asked us to write down a dream we've had on hold. I wrote down that I wanted to write a book. Yvonne had mentioned that she had authored six books, so I approached her after the session (along with a relatively large group of people!) and let her know that my Getting Unstuck dream was to write a book. She offered to stay in touch and gave me her business card. So, what did I do? You guessed it! I followed up, and we talked about my book idea—which she loved. We decided to collaborate on the book and became fast friends.

   My advice: *When you exchange contact information or business cards, write down the plan for following up or the commitment you made when you spoke to make sure that you remember what you said once you get home with a potentially large pile of business cards. For example, I promised to phone this person to make plans to have a coffee together.*

3. **Joining a co-working space for women:**

   I joined a co-working space for women shortly after attending a holiday market hosted at the venue. I loved the energy of collaboration and inspiration. The women I met at the space were motivated and fun to talk to. I have since made amazing friends through the online and in-person events I attended through the co-working space.

One of my closest friends, Mila, and I met at one of the events hosted in the space. Another friend, Courtney, messaged me on Instagram after seeing me on the virtual community calls. She reached out and said that she'd love to connect over a Zoom call. So, we did, and she and I have been cheering each other on ever since.

My advice: *See if there are any co-working spaces near you. They might have a community membership or host events you can attend.*

There are even options to connect with people through a virtual co-working membership. As you try new things, you will eventually find a sweet spot for the events that make it easy and enjoyable for you to meet people.

4. **A phone app to meet new friends:**

When my friends were all paired up and spending lots of time with their significant others, I decided to actively meet some new people. So, I joined Bumble BFF: a phone application that helps people find new friends. Cassandra and I "matched" over a shared love of karaoke. We spent time together, went out on the town, and had a lot of fun! She dropped off after she started dating someone seriously (ironically), but I still highly recommend Bumble BFF as a great way to make new friends.

My advice: *When joining an application for making friends, start slow so you don't get overwhelmed. Try getting to know one new person to start.*

5. **Reconnecting with a friend from high school:**

When I moved to a new city for work, I made a post on Facebook to let my network know I had moved and asked if anyone else was currently located in the city. A woman I was friends with in high school, Brandi, reached out and told me that she lives in the city and would love to get together. So, we did! Many, many Bachelor nights later, it was as though no time had passed between us. We ended up as closer friends than we had been in high school.

My advice: *You can use social media to let people know you are new in town. You can also post the date of a concert or event you'd like to attend with a note asking if anyone is interested in attending with you. For example, "I want to go see Ed Sheeran in concert. Would anyone like to join me?" If you're worried that someone you don't want to attend the concert with replies to your post, remember that you can exclude certain people from seeing your posts. You can also review your privacy settings and delete or block people from your social media if you don't want to stay connected with them.*

6. **Volunteering to work on a community television program:**

I was a friend's guest at a gala and started chatting with my friend's friend at the event. She learned that I was Polish, so she introduced me to a group of her Polish friends at the event. One of the ladies and I started talking, and I found out that she produced and hosted a community television program. I told her I would love to volunteer my help. She was thrilled! I started working on the program with her, and when she left the show, I put up an ad to get some more volunteers. Camila answered the ad, and we started working together. We both eventually moved out of the city and didn't stay in touch regularly, but she reached out to me again when I started working as a career coach. She hired me, and we picked up where we left off in our friendship.

My advice: *There are websites where you can see volunteer opportunities in your city or town. These are great because they make it easier to find something you enjoy and allow you to utilize your unique talents. Over the years, I've volunteered on the board of an organization I care about, a community theatre for one of their productions, and a nature centre helping with programs for children.*

7. **Attending a party for my colleague:**

   I became friends with one of my colleagues by initiating lunchtime plans. She invited me to her karaoke birthday party (my favourite type of birthday party!), and I stayed in touch with one of the women I met at her party after asking for her contact information and following up. Two years later, she is one of my closest friends, and we are each other's biggest cheerleaders.

   My advice: *People have different approaches to making friends in the workplace. It's usually easiest to form friendships with people at work who work in lateral roles. When trying to build on a connection, be mindful of how someone responds to an invitation to go for lunch or have coffee. If someone seems hesitant or delays the plans, they might not be open to friendships at work. Allow people to set boundaries where they need to. There will be others who are interested in making friends. Remember not to take someone's approach to work relationships personally.*

Those are some unique ways I have added to my friend group. Feel free to try at least one of these methods if you are interested in making new friends!

A Guide for Introverts

You might be thinking, "I am not an outgoing person. There is no way I would be able to approach people this easily and be clear and direct about my intentions to stay in touch." When you're shy about making new friends or approaching people, taking some uncertainty out of the situation is helpful. We often feel fearful because we are unsure if the other person is interested in making a new friend.

For those of you who would like some strategies that work well for those who are shy, I have compiled the following list:

1. Meetup.com is a website where people can form groups based on various interests. There are groups for people who want to play soccer, learn to cook, go hiking, explore the city they live in, have bake-offs, and go boating. There are so many options! Of course, if the activity you are interested in doesn't have a group in your city, you can start one by yourself or with a friend. Meetup.com is a great way to make new friends for a few reasons:

    - People join these groups because they are interested in making new friends. It removes the guesswork around whether the person you meet is looking to meet new people.

    - It is less intimidating to meet new people when the event is centred around an activity. Because the activity creates opportunities for discussion and interaction, you don't have to worry about what to say.

    - It's a great way to meet people who have a common interest. Regardless of how many friends we have, when we develop a new interest that our current friends don't enjoy or want to partake in, meet-ups are a great way to explore our new interests and meet people who can share them with us.

2. Another way to make new friends is to pair up with an outgoing friend who is skilled at starting conversations and making new friends. You can join a meet-up group or attend a party with them and let them know in advance that you'd love their help connecting with new friends when you're there.

3. It's sometimes easier to make friends with someone you already know. Most people also have a network of acquaintances that could become possible friendships. Make a list of people you know that you might enjoy getting to know better.

   Regardless of your approach, it is key to remember why you would like to make new friends. Your motivation will ebb and flow, especially when fear is involved. Your fears will say, "I love spending time with myself—I don't need more friends," or "I enjoy spending time with people I know well, not people I don't know at all!"

We typically take action when our need exceeds our fear, but we can consciously tap into our motivation. Take the time to write down the reasons why you want to make new friends and refer to them when your motivation wanes and Netflix beckons. When you've identified a need or desire for more friends, but you don't act on it, take the time to examine why and unpack any fears that might be buried underneath. A richness can be added to your life when you reach out and connect with others.

It's also important to note that there are many introverts with a full social circle and many extroverts with many connections but a few meaningful friendships. Try not to idealize the life of an extrovert. You bring a lot of great qualities to the table.

If you're an extrovert without many close friends, list those people in your network that you would like to get to know better and reach out to one. Center your plans on an activity that allows you to connect effectively. For example, a nature walk is sometimes a better choice than an outing to your local pub because you have the opportunity to get to know each other without distractions.

Key Learning

- If you want to make new friends, don't let your fears get the best of you. Lots of people are looking for new friends, too.
- You can make friends in unexpected ways if you stay mindful of your goal and aware of the opportunities around you.
- Introverts may approach friendship-making differently.

Discussion Questions

1. Are you interested in making new friends? Why or why not?
2. How can you add more friends to your network or deepen relationships with those who might contribute to your sense of fulfillment and happiness?
3. How did you meet your newest friend?
4. Are there particular qualities you want to have in a new friend? How might you ensure that your new friend has these qualities?
5. Are there specific interests you would like to have in common with your friend?
6. What's one way of making new friends you would like to try in the next month?

Celebrating our Female Friendships

"My life is better because you're in it."

We started this book celebrating the joys of female friendships, and we will end it just the same. Despite the ups and downs, the challenges, the sometimes-hazy role expectations, and even the conflicts, those who have benefited from having girlfriends in our lives consider it a great privilege.

We asked, "If you were asked to write a tribute for one of your most treasured female friends, what would you say?" 95% of our respondents had much to say. Good things. Some of their comments have been scattered generously throughout the preceding chapters, but we leave you with the tributes they wrote—pithy sayings or longer treatises that go straight to the heart of this book.

Tributes

We did not begin together as best friends. That took time and maturity. At one time, I think I was the giver and you the recipient, but we have received equally with time. You have supported me during many life changes, marriage, pregnancies (especially when you could not), career changes, etc. You have encouraged my dreams and tried to promote what I do. You tell me that I am important to you, and though we do not meet or speak weekly or daily, our annual or bi-annual weekends away provide such high-quality catching up and bolstering that I look forward to them each year with great anticipation. Thank you for being the wind beneath my wings.

**

Ola, I appreciate your huge heart, patience, and steady love for me. I cannot imagine going through life without your encouragement, love, and all our amazing talks.

**

I value you. I appreciate you and all that you've done to and for me. I am not the same person without you. My life is better because you're in it.

**

Thank you for standing by me and always being there for me. Love you!

**

You are one of the most important people in my life, and I am so grateful for you. Your intelligence, compassion, sense of fun, and loyalty make you invaluable to me!

**

Thank you for being the wind at my back in the good and bad times. You have been on the path with me through life's journey for 37 wonderful years, and I wouldn't trade you for anyone. We have learned and grown through the many challenges and obstacles, but one thing that never changes is the love, trust, and respect that we hold near and dear for each other. You will always be my ride-or-die bestie.

**

You're a fighter, and I know it's because nobody fought for you. Just know I'll fight for you. I love you.

**

I treasure our friendship more than I can express. We've known each other for over 40 years and have never had a disagreement or argument. I value our relationship and the time we both have invested in it. I think about how we used to do everything together. Even though life has brought about certain changes—children, grandchildren, travelling, etc.—our friendship has stayed the same and will remain strong. What makes you so special to me, my friend, is that I can trust you no matter what. You are kind, considerate, honest, patient, and loyal, among other qualities. You have accomplished so much in your life. I appreciate you and who you have become, both as a friend and mother and grandmother. I have seen where, time and time again, you have sacrificed your life for your grandchildren, whom you care for so lovingly and generously—no matter how tired you are! Also, again, thank you for the sacrifice you made in making it possible for my husband to finally reunite with me. That act of selflessness will never be forgotten. Thank you! Thank you! Thank you! I love you always!!

**

You motivate me every day to want to do better. Thanks for not judging me when I judge myself. When I'm down, you are always there to pick me up, encourage me, and listen; even when I don't want to talk, you are still there, even to sit in silence. For this friendship, I am forever grateful. Your patience and strength as a mother are incredible. Love your organizational skills and love how we work well as a team. Love you always!

**

You picked me up, nursed, walked with, listened to, and taught me how to be a best friend.

**

Your friendship over the years has brought me many happy, comforting, and uplifting moments—not to mention the crazy, funny exchanges we've shared. You are among my most loved and valued relationships. Your strength has lifted me even when I wasn't there for you. Your words comforted me even when they were hard to hear. Your spirituality helped to guide me when my faith wavered. And not to be forgotten is your funny, wacky, zany flipside, which always shows up at the right time.

**

I love our friendship because both of us speak our minds. No matter how silly the things we say and do may be, we can laugh with each other and not be offended. I know you will always be there for me if I ever call upon you, and I hope you know I will be here for you.

**

My sisters, my friends, when God created us, he knew that we needed each other and allowed us to meet through Divine intervention. Your love for the Lord and others inspires me, and I thank the Lord for your friendship.

**

I came to Canada not knowing what to expect, only that I wanted a better life. It was rough initially, but I thank God for you every day. You showed up when I needed you the most. Thank you for always looking out for me and opening your heart and wallet for me, a stranger! I tell this story to so many people because I believe you are an angel among us. You are like a mother to me. I love you, and I am truly grateful for all you do.

**

You make me a better person.

**

You mean a lot to me.

**

I appreciate your good humour and your unstoppable zest for life and love. Even in the face of adversity, you find the good and consistently care for others—whether expressed through a painting, food, humour, or words. You listen to others and empathize with them, even when in pain. You are strong beyond measure, and I am lucky to be your friend.

**

I appreciate your friendship and never want to lose you.

**

You have been there when I needed a friend. Your words and actions raised me when life's trials seem to have no end. I did not expect perfection from you, and yes, you were an excellent friend. I remember when you had to bend, send, lend, mend, and tend. You have been a wonderful friend. Thanks for being my friend.

**

My actions have always been louder than my words. Love is an action word. I choose you every time.

**

Thank you for sticking by me all these years, listening to me, motivating me when I felt like giving up on certain things, and just being in my life because I honestly couldn't imagine it without you. We don't talk every day or see each other often, but it's like no time has passed when we do. Nothing will ever change how I feel about you because we've come this far and have much further to go.

**

You inspire me and always make me want to be a better person.

**

Thank you for always believing in and supporting me no matter what.

**

Thank you for always having my back. Thank you for loving my family and me. Thank you for always listening and encouraging me to follow through. Thank you for being supportive of my choices. Thank you for always offering sound advice. I love you!

**

You are the rock that I tie myself to in stormy seas.

**

Your smile is the window to make anyone feel special every day. Thank you for your compassion and "real talk" that encourages me to analyze my decisions. Your endless support in my life is a testament to our deep ties and bonds. I appreciate you for who you are and everything you have brought to help enhance who I am.

**

I love you dearly. You have been there for me since the beginning of time, and even though distance has separated us, it's just like old times when we connect. The way we still think and share the same values is sometimes uncanny, but I love it. When you find a true friend, you really find a soul mate akin to you. You are that individual, and I thank God for bringing us together as he did and allowing our relationship to grow into a beautiful union.

**

Thank you for knowing what I need and being there when I need it.

**

I love you without condition. I would like to support you when you have challenging times.

**

Thank you for being my sister. Thank you for loving my children like they were yours. Thank you for not being judgemental when I shared unsavoury things about myself. Thank you for teaching me poise when I wanted to fight in the streets. And thank you for being the strong, loving, caring person I've always looked up to.

**

I genuinely love you and our relationship. You have been there for me when I needed you, and I would be very disappointed if our friendship could not continue.

**

You're awesome. You make life great because you exist.

**

Thank you for the love and laughter you have brought into my life! I feel so blessed to have met you and got to know you. I'm so happy to have a friendship with someone who really sees me as a person. I feel very motivated and uplifted by our friendship. I hope we always try and work things out and help each other grow. I love you!

**

You're one of the most intrinsically good people I've ever met. I'm lucky to have you as a friend, and the world is a better place because you're in it.

**

You are strong, smart, and successful—Woman, Wife, Mother, Nurse, Christian. You care so much for others that you deserve to be spoiled for the rest of your life. Thanks for being there, and for being open and willing to share your life experiences and give advice. Thanks for respecting my boundaries when I didn't want to talk or couldn't reach out. Thanks for your friendship. Thank you for YOU!

**

I thank God for placing you in my life at the perfect time. Words can't express enough what you mean to me or our growth together. Love you, girl!

**

Thank you sincerely for understanding and never trying to pressure me into your ideal of what I should be.

**

We have shared so much over the years. Your laughter is from your "belly bottom." Your tears were mine, as well. You know me from the inside out and have allowed me to know you. I can't count your qualities—they're endless. Thank you for being more than a friend to me.

**

I know I haven't been as good of a friend as I should have been. Thank you for not giving up on me. I'll do better in the future.

**

You're one of the most wonderful people I have ever met. Your courage amazes me, and I love that you love God. May God continue to bless you.

**

A truly dependable friend is everything—and to me, that friend is you.

**

You are confident and full of life, love, and wisdom. You helped me learn and see so much, and I hope you will stay in my life forever.

**

Thank you for being there to celebrate the smallest of wins to the darkest of tunnels that didn't have a light. You've made it bearable and better as we continue this enduring path of life together. Thank you for never giving up on us.

**

I could not have lived my best life without you!

**

You influenced me to be a better person and made every day with you worth living. The fun times we had changed my life.

**

I told one of my close friends this a while ago: I feel like we're soul friends. We don't see each other as much as we'd like, but I feel a deep, almost spiritual connection every time we hang out.

**

I am blessed beyond belief to have you in my life. I am grateful every day we met because if it were not for you and what you bring to my life, I would not be the person I am today. Thank you for your support, love, and honesty. I promise to always be the same to you and be myself in whatever way I can. Never, ever compromise your self-worth or value for anyone! You are an amazing friend (more like a family member), and I will forever be so lucky to have you in my life.

**

Your self-awareness is so inspiring.

**

Thank you for being my truest friend. The person I am the most myself around because I know that you are a judgement-free zone. The person I laugh the hardest with because the more ridiculous we are, the funnier it becomes. You accept and support your friends just like they were your family. You want the best for people and are always willing to share your time, space, resources, advice, etc. You try to make people feel special and loved, especially on birthdays. You spotlight your friends' best moments. You never try to make things about yourself or steal anyone else's fire. You are the best listener. You are clever and hilarious and have the best one-liners.

**

You have given me unconditional love, and for that, I am eternally grateful!

**

Thank you for being you. You make my life better and lift up my heart. You helped me love myself when I didn't always know how to. Thank you. I love you. You will always have a place in my heart.

**

Thank you for being a hilarious, kind, and deeply weird person.

**

Thank you for seeing me through my darkest days and my greatest joys. It has been so much fun to live this life with you. I am lucky to call you a friend.

**

You have always stood by me. You kept in touch even though we are now on opposite sides of the planet. I know I can trust you always.

**

I am so grateful to have someone in my life that keeps me grounded, where the support is mutual, and there is so much honesty. I appreciate having kind people like you around me that inspire me with their talents. Your giving nature and listening ear have been a blessing, especially when I was at my lowest. Despite being apart, I'm grateful we can keep the bond of our friendship so strong, without pressure, knowing we'll be there for each other regardless of where our lives take us.

**

Thank you so much for everything you have done for me. You were there for me during my happy and sad times. I specifically remember how you got two other acquaintances to sing at my wedding. That took a big load off my back and gave me time to concentrate on other things. I love you dearly and will never forget your thoughtfulness and kindness. Thank you, my friend.

**

I love you. You are an incredible sister and friend. You are generous beyond measure, and your presence makes this world better.

**

You're stronger and smarter than you think and should try harder to be content.

**

You need to let go and be the person you are with us, your closest confidants, and share that with the world. You are smart, witty, nurturing, beautiful, creative, and down-to-earth. People may think you are guarded or cold, but it couldn't be further from the truth.

**

I adore you so much for always being a big sister and guiding me even when I was bratty and unkind.

**

Thank you for always being an ear and providing advice during rough times

**

You've always been in my life, and I am super proud of the person you have become.

**

God wants me to have you in my life.

**

Wow! Did you not feel choked up over some of these tributes?! We love being loved. We love being seen. We love the girlfriend who 'gets us.' Call her a supporter, a cheerleader, and a constant. She is empowering, encouraging, and enduring for a season, for a reason, and even for a lifetime. With her, we can be so much more of our authentic selves. No apologies.

Sisters from the same or another mother, we salute you for what you do every day to enrich the lives of the women you share space with. Keep loving and living with tenacious joy and feisty abandon. You inspire us to shine our lights a lot brighter.

Discussion Questions

1. What tribute would you write to your friend(s)? What would you be most appreciative of?
2. Do your close female friends know how much they mean to you?
3. Are you comfortable communicating how you feel to your female friends?
4. What is one thing you could do to enrich your current friendships?
5. What is one thing you would like from your female friend(s) that would enrich your life?

Afterthoughts

Yvonne

A long time ago, someone introduced me to the statement that awareness is the key to change. Without awareness, we are fated to keep making the same mistakes repeatedly. With awareness, there is the possibility of insight; from insight, we can examine ways to shift, change, and reposition ourselves for the better. So how is this relevant?

Yesterday, as my daughter and I ran errands, she started filling me in on the weekend she had spent with her girlfriends. These four young women are in their mid-twenties and have known each other since childhood. They get together at least every two months to catch up, spend time, bond, and eat.

As she recounted their recent weekend activities, I asked her, "What role do you play in the group?" And I followed that up with, "Did you choose that role or fall into it?"

She mentioned that she and another woman in their quad group are the organizers and implementers. She does not see herself as the group leader but as the one who executes the plan once a decision is made to do something. She described her other two friends as the co-operators, but not the initiators. If the leader championed an idea or indicated she would participate, the others tended to fall in line with her (I suspect at some level that my daughter wishes that these 'co-operator' friends would do things with her even if the 'leader' could not participate).

As I listened to our conversation, I had this "Aha" moment. Our discussion and the information I was sharing grew out of the material in this book. None of it is revolutionary but rather profoundly insightful.

Writing this book, and hearing from other women on the topic of female friendships, gave me a new level of awareness about the dynamics at play in female friendships. It helped me see things and voice things that I knew but could not always articulate. It provided language.

Emilia

As Yvonne and I wrote this book, my observations, experiences, and opinions evolved. The last year has been transformative for many of my friendships. Some beginning, some deepening, some ending, and some lying dormant as we navigate a global pandemic.

The biggest lesson—and the one I hope to leave you all with—is that your friendships will change. Your life will change, your friends' lives will change, and these changes can create challenges from time to time. If you allow yourself to ease into the changes, get curious about them, and flow with them, your friendships will evolve and maintain their resilience. If you resist the changes in your friendships as your lives change, you will become frustrated. Your friendships will either stagnate, fall apart, or suffer a slow death. This is probably the most important lesson that my 30s have brought me so far.

The writing of this book began with a question: How can we strengthen and build our friendships? Here's the answer: Be gentle with yourself and your friends. Your friendships will not always look a certain way but stay open to what they could look like and hold an intention to nurture your female friendships with each chapter of your life.

And so, we've come full circle: from examining to writing to examining again. Celebrating the women in our lives who continue to bolster and support us. And examining the relationships that don't.

Our take-away from this guide is increased awareness. With this increased awareness, we can look at our friendships through a more transparent lens. It might fire us up to start a conversation on roles, expectations, or other topics that resonated from reading this book.

We trust that you will experience this newfound awareness so your female friendships can continue growing and thriving.

Let the Conversation Continue: Friendship Circles

Wouldn't it be great if we could take some of the content from this guide to create online and in-person discussion groups?

We do!

Groups for sharing and hearing stories, laughing, crying, thinking, analyzing, and growing. This is what we love to do as women when we get together.

If you would like to be part of our Friendship Circles, email Emilia at ***femalefriendshipguide@gmail.com.***

Your voice and perspective are welcomed and appreciated!

And it's gonna be a whole lotta fun!

About the Authors

Emilia Stypulkowska holds a bachelor's degree in Rhetoric and Professional Writing. Her career has spanned non-profit work, fundraising, and consulting to running her business as a career coach. She loves learning about people, having deep conversations, and nurturing her relationships. As a coach, she loves helping women gain the confidence they need to pursue their dreams and desires. Emilia hails from Poland. She is in her 30s and lives with her partner in the GTA.

Yvonne Rodney holds a master's degree in Counselling Psychology from the University of Toronto and is an author, counsellor, speaker, and playwright. Yvonne loves to find creative ways to tackle complex issues in her stage plays or books. To date, she's written six books: *Getting Through, Let it Go, The Waiting Heart, Curse God & Die, Military to Civilian Employment: A Career Practitioner's Guide, and Melanie's Decision.* She has also produced many stage plays within the city of Toronto.

Yvonne divides her time between her consulting practice, Inner Change Consulting, which provides coaching to individuals and organizations in career and personal development, her speaking engagements and writing, and career counselling at a Toronto-based agency.

Section 1 of 8

Appendix A: Female Friendship Questionnaire

All reference to friendships in this questionnaire are about female friendships and should be answered as such

Email Address* ____________________

After section 1 Continue to next section

Section 2 of 8

Respondent profile

Description (optional)

Name *

____

Age Bracket *

- ○ 20-30
- ○ 30-40
- ○ 40-50
- ○ 50-60
- ○ 60-70
- ○ 70+

Ethnic background

____

After section 2 Continue to next section

Section 3 of 8

Friendship criteria

All reference to friendships in the questionnaire are about female friendships and should be answered by such

Looking at your life now, how many women would you say are really close friend?

___

What qualities do you treasure in your close friends?

___

Thinking about a best friend that you now have or one in the past, how long have you been friends?

___

How did you get to be best friends?

___

Think about your newest female friends—how did you meet them? (Select all that apply).

- ☐ Work
- ☐ Religious group
- ☐ Volunteering
- ☐ Social event
- ☐ Travelling
- ☐ Online
- ☐ Throughout mutual friend
- ☐ Conference/networking event
- ☐ Through family
- ☐ Other ...

On a scale of 1 to 5, with 5 being the easiest, how easy do you find it to make new friends as an adult?

	1	2	3	4	5	
Very difficult	○	○	○	○	○	Very easy

If you answered 3 or below to the question above, describe what makes it difficult to make new friends.

____

Are you interested in making new friends?

- ○ Yes
- ○ No
- ○ Maybe

What factors have influenced your female friendship choices? (Select your top 3).

- ☐ Shared interest
- ☐ Shared values
- ☐ Compatible personlaity
- ☐ Admiration
- ☐ Shared history
- ☐ Feeling valued/accepted
- ☐ Similar life stage
- ☐ Proximity
- ☐ Friend of significant other
- ☐ Feeling of being understood
- ☐ Other ...

Was there a defining moment or event that served as a catalyst to solidify one or more of your friendships?

- ○ Yes
- ○ No

If you answered 'Yes' to the above, explain why.

____

In your opinion, what are the benefits of female friendships?

After section 3 Continue to next section

Section 4 of 8

Maintaining relationship(s): roles, expectation, pockets, cross-pollination ...

All reference to friendships in the questionnaire are about female friendships and should be answered by such

What role(s) do you assume in your friendships (Select your top 2)

- ☐ Cooperator/obliger
- ☐ Peacemaker/conciliator
- ☐ Initiator
- ☐ Correspondent
- ☐ Supporter/cheerleader
- ☐ Provacateur/disturber
- ☐ Confronter

Pertaining to the previous question, do you play the same role in every friendship?

- ○ Yes
- ○ No

How do you feel about the role you play within your friendships? (Select the 1 that most apply).

- ○ Happy with my role
- ○ Mostly ok with my role
- ○ Resentful
- ○ Tolerate my role
- ○ Others...

Do you generally verbalize or discuss your expectations of each other for your friendships?

- ○ Yes
- ○ No

How secure do you feel in your really close friendship (s)?

- ☐ Very secure
- ☐ Mostly secure
- ☐ Somewhat secure
- ☐ Insecure
- ☐ Very insecure
- ☐ Depends on which friendship
- ☐ Other ...

What contributes to your feeling of security in a friendship

____

Author Gary Chapman in his book "The Five Love Languages" describes 5 main types of love. Which of the following describes your top 2 love languages?

- ☐ Acts of service (ex. assists with tasks)
- ☐ Words of affirmation (ex. tells you they love you)
- ☐ Receiving gifts
- ☐ Quality time
- ☐ Physical touch (ex. hugging)
- ☐ Other...

Which method do you use most to stay in touch with your close femal friends?

- ○ In person meet-up
- ○ Direct messaging/text
- ○ Video (eg. Facetime. Zoom)
- ○ Group chat
- ○ Email
- ○ Snail mail
- ○ Phone calls
- ○ Other...

How frequently do you communicate with your close femal friends?

- ○ Daily
- ○ Weekly
- ○ Monthly
- ○ Yearly
- ○ Other...

If the frequency of communication with your close friend(s) have changed over the years, how so?

____

Do you have friendship pockets (a cluster of friends)?

- ○ Yes
- ○ No

Do you allow your friendship pockets to meet each other

- ○ Yes
- ○ No
- ○ Occasionally

If you answer 'No' to the above, why not?

____

After section 4 Continue to next section

Section 5 of 8

Life events: Impact on friendships

All reference to friendships in the questionnaire are about female friendships and should be answered by such

Have any of the following life event have negatively impacted your close friendships? (Select all that apply)

- ☐ Marraige/commited relationship (yours or your friend's)
- ☐ Parenting
- ☐ Divorce/breakups
- ☐ Loss/death
- ☐ Wedding participation
- ☐ Other...

If applicable, provide an example of how one of the above life events negatively affected your relationship with close friend and how you navigated the transition?

____

Was there ever a time when you or a close friend have to move away from each other?

- ○ Yes
- ○ No

If you answered Yes to the above, descrive the impact of the move on your relationship...

____

After section 5 Continue to next section

Which of the following ways describe how typically you handly conflicts or disagreements on your close friendships?

- ○ I ignore conflicts
- ○ I tend to drop pointed hints
- ○ I address it directly and immediately
- ○ I think things through then address it
- ○ I vent to other friends
- ○ Other...

Describe a particular conflict or disagreement that troubled your relationship with a close friend...

____

When (if) there is conflict between 2 or more member for your friend group, how does it usually play out?

____

If you made a new friend that resulted in feelings of jealousy on the part of an existing close friend, describe how you delat with it ...

____

If you find that you are the one consistently investing more time, energy and resource in a friendship without reciprocity, how would you deal with the imbalance? (Select you usual response)

- ○ Discuss it head-on
- ○ Drop hints
- ○ Suffer in silence
- ○ Complain to other people
- ○ Sever the friendship
- ○ Invest less/pull back
- ○ Other...

Have your close framale friends ever done anything to make you feel left out?

- ○ Yes
- ○ No

If you answered Yes to the above what, if anything, did you do about it?

____

After section 6 Continue to next section

Section 7 of 8

Letting go

All reference to friendships in the questionnaire are about female friendships and should be answered by such

If you've ever decided to sever ties with a friend, which of the following options did you employ?

- ☐ Stopped all communication
- ☐ Inform the person of decision

- [ ] Gradually reduced contact and communication
- [ ] Came up with excuses not to meet
- [ ] Other...

In assessing your current female friendshi, is there 1 or more that you're thinking you should let go?

- ○ Yes
- ○ No

If you answered Yes to the above, what are your taking into consideration before making a decision?

____

After section 7 Continue to next section

Section 8 of 8

Words of wisdom

All reference to friendships in the questionnaire are about female friendships and should be answered by such

What are the important lessons you've learned over the years about femals friendship?

____

Knowing what you are know now, what's the best advise you'd give to a younger woman about female friendship?

____

If asked to write a tribute to one of your most treasured friends, what would you say to that person?

____

Appendix A: Questionnaire

All reference to friendships in the questionnaire are about female friendships and should be answered by such

Printed in Dunstable, United Kingdom

63575088R00090